FROM:-

Lucy. Donny

TO MR. BOLLEN ON HIS
63 BIRTHDAY.

Toothy Goes To War

The author

Toothy Goes To War

Memoirs of a Dental Officer
1939–46

by
Robert Bagshaw

To

Nicholas and Sue

"When first my way to fair I took
Few pence in purse had I,
And long I used to stand and look
At things I could not buy.

Now times are altered; if I care
To buy a thing, I can;
The pence are here and here's the fair
But where's the lost young man?"

A.E. Housman.

ISBN   Hardback: 0 900616 24 5
        Paperback: 0 900616 25 3

        Printed and published by
        Geo. R. Reeve Ltd., Damgate, Wymondham, Norfolk

Contents

Illustrations

Introduction

An earlier book* followed the fortunes of the little boy who, born in Cromer, grew up in the Norfolk countryside in the years between the wars. It was a time of much poverty and deprivation as the country struggled to regain normality after four years of conflict, but his was an uncluttered childhood, for life was simple and undemanding. Above all, it was an age in which nothing ever seemed to change, yet one which has now become little more than a memory.

The previous book gave, in the words of one reviewer, "a picture of early century life as seen through the eyes of a sensitive, impressionable youngster". The pages which now follow, however, tell a totally different story, for the little country boy, having achieved the status of a teenager, was suddenly to find himself thrust into manhood without experiencing the long-awaited promises of youth. He was one of a generation who were too young to vote but old enough to fight.

Even under normal conditions, the sudden transfer from the quiet Norfolk countryside to the grimy squalor of London's East End would not have come easily to the youngster who, hitherto, had rarely crossed the boundary of his own county. Living amongst a strange race of people and studying in a vast general hospital would have been daunting enough in peacetime. The fact that his arrival in Whitechapel coincided with the outbreak of the Second World War merely served to increase the difficulties which lay ahead.

The next four years were hardly conducive to a tranquil life. Daily studying went on against a background of rationing and restriction, of bombing and destruction. Then, having achieved professional status, there were to come a further four years as a Dental Officer in the Royal Navy. If the nightly slaughter on the streets of London had not already done so, this latter period was destined to bring an acute realisation of the futility of War.

In spite of the tragedy and suffering of those long years of conflict, however, life was not without its compensations. Many people, thrown together by the force of circumstances, forged

Poppies to Paston   7

lasting friendships with others whom they otherwise might never have met. The people of London, cowering in their underground shelters during the nightly bombardments, shared a bond of sympathy with fellow-sufferers who, until then, had been complete strangers. Above all, they suddenly found that they had a sense of humour.

Vera Lynn kept singing, Winston Churchill poured forth his rousing speeches, and the King stubbornly refused to be driven out of Buckingham Palace. And, all the while, the ordinary folk lifted their spirits with jokes about Hitler and Goebbels, Ribbentrop and Mussolini, and anything else which they considered worthy of their derision. Above all, irrespective of class or social status, they were united. It is, perhaps, a sad reflection on the frailty of human nature that it should have taken a calamity of such magnitude to develop in the people of Britain the unity of purpose which suddenly came to the fore.

It has always been a matter of some regret to me that I was never able to savour the so-called pleasures of youth. In compensation, however, I lived through those years in the company of men and women from all walks of life who, whether as servicemen or civilians, forged a common bond out of adversity and developed a unified determination to see the thing through to the bitter end. It was, indeed, a privilege.

Robert Bagshaw
Wymondham, Norfolk. 1987

8

CHAPTER 1

The Reason Why

The decision that I should become a dentist was not one of my making. I was brought up in the Norfolk countryside in an age when such things were decided by one's parents, and the thought of questioning such a decision would never have crossed my mind. There can be little doubt that, if the choice had been left to me, dentistry would have come very low on my list of preferences, for it was a somewhat unpopular profession. It was, furthermore, a very young profession, for it was only in 1921 that an Act of Parliament had debarred all but the properly trained from carrying out treatment on the public. For many centuries before that, sufferers had, of necessity, to throw themselves upon the mercy of a variety of practitioners in order to gain relief.

In country districts the extraction of teeth was carried out by such tradesmen as blacksmiths and shoemakers as well as by chemists and rural doctors. Parson Woodforde, the diarist, recorded an occasion when he had to call in the village farrier to extract a tooth for him. Every barber, of course, combined tooth-drawing and blood-letting with his other activities, a fact well advertised by the striped pole of red and white which he displayed outside his premises. Then there were the itinerant operators who were a great attraction at markets and fairs, signalling their presence with loud music which also served to drown the cries of their patients. In my early years I met a number of people who, within their lifetime, had witnessed such carryings-on. Little wonder, then, that the profession I was to enter could not, at that time, be truly described as an attractive one in the eyes of the general public.

It was not any kind of medical background which led to my parents' decision as to my future, for we lived in a world of journalism and the Press. My eldest brother, however, had become a dental surgeon and, as he and I were generally regarded as being in many ways similar beings, it was reckoned that I would follow in his footsteps. Fortunately for me, my future was decided at a very early age and what began as passive acceptance of my destiny gradually acquired a far greater significance in my young mind

9

THE COUNTRY TOOTH DRAWER.

An eighteenth century farrier grips his pincers with both hands as he struggles to remove an aching tooth. His patient retaliates by grabbing his nose!

until, by the time I had left school, it had become the over-riding ambition in my life. At the age of sixteen I knew that dentistry was the profession to which I wanted to devote my working life, and at no time in the years that followed was I to have cause to regret my decision.

I applied myself to the task of passing the Pre-Medical Examination which was necessary for acceptance at a teaching hospital and, at the same time, I found employment in a dental laboratory in Norwich. Not only did this provide me with certain skills which would later be of advantage to me, but I also received financial reward for my efforts. In the first year I received five shillings per week and then I was given an increase of half-a-crown, although this was later withdrawn when I asked for time off on Saturday mornings to attend biology classes.

Success in the necessary examinations was only one of the pre-requisites for acceptance at a teaching hospital, for one then had to undergo an interview with the Dean of one's chosen college. To me, the choice of hospital was automatic – it had to be the London. My brother had been trained there, as had several other people of my acquaintance. One heard a lot about the glamour of Guy's, or Bart's or St. Mary's, but to any old Londoner there is only one hospital worth considering. I say this with all due respect to graduates of other establishments who, I am sure, feel the same about their own alma mater. To me, however, it was the London and, accordingly, I applied for an interview.

The London Hospital had a long and ancient heritage, stretching back over two centuries to the days when there was no such thing as an organised medical profession. It had been built in 1760 in what were then the green fields of Whitechapel. Twenty-five years later it was considered that its situation, "far removed from the places of dissipation", would be ideal for the establishment of a medical college. Thus began the institution within whose walls I was hoping to gain admittance.

As the years went by, the face of Britain was destined to be transformed by the demands of the Industrial Revolution, and nowhere was this more dramatic than in the countryside around London. In Whitechapel, in particular, the green fields were swept away as the tentacles of industry pushed ever outward. Soon the rolling countryside had become nothing less than the East End of London, with its teeming mass of people and their ever-increasing demands for medical care. The hospital expanded to meet the challenge and, by the middle of the nineteenth century, was able to boast of being the largest voluntary hospital in England. This, indeed, was a position it was to hold with pride until 1948, when it became part of the National Health Service.

At the time of my hoped-for arrival, the London had more than 800 beds and served not only as the district general hospital for the local population but also as a treatment centre to which patients were referred from all parts of the country. Above all, however, it stood as a symbol of humanity both to the folk who lived in the little streets around it and to the people who worked within its walls. I looked forward to the day when I might count myself among their number.

The day of my interview duly arrived and it was necessary to make an early start for the trip to London. My brother had offered to drive me there in his little Austin Seven Ruby Saloon, known to all the family (to his great disgust) as "The Puddlejumper".

Motoring was a much more leisurely occupation in those days, for it was before the arrival of motorways and extensive bypass routes. The A11 was a pleasant country road where traffic ambled along past green verges and through countless little country villages.

An alfresco meal near Audley End in the days when the A11 was a quiet country thoroughfare.

Very few drivers were in too much of a hurry and, when one felt the need for refreshment, it was possible simply to pull in onto the grass at some chosen spot and bring out the sandwiches and thermos flask. This we did at a quiet spot near Audley End, sitting on the running board of the car as we shared our repast. Then it was on through Newport and Quendon, Ugley and Epping, and it was all rather like a pleasant little run out in the country. Gradually, however, things began to change and it was as we neared the outer fringes of London that I realised we were entering another world.

Leytonstone was not too much of a shock, but then came Stratford, Bow and Stepney. There the change in our surroundings was dramatic in the extreme and, as we ambled along towards Whitechapel, the transformation was complete. This was my first real introduction to London's East End and, although I had heard descriptions of the district, I was completely unprepared for what I saw. All around us there were drab factory buildings and warehouses, whilst each side of the road was tightly lined with a multitude of little businesses of every imagineable type. There were chemists and greengrocers, tobacconists and clothiers, all seemingly packed in by the dozen. Then there were strange establishments offering such things as jellied eels and kosher food, which was something I had never before encountered, and most of them bore strange-sounding names which obviously owed much to their Jewish origins. Even the people in the streets had a strange look about them which marked them out as being somewhat different from the folk amongst whom I had spent my earlier years. Above all, however, the entire area gave me an impression of unpleasing ugliness combined with an inexplicable air of hustle and bustle.

I was just trying to come to terms with the fact that this was where I was expected to spend the next few years of my life when, on the left, the object of our journey came into view. There stood the hospital, extending its massive frontage along a vast length of Whitechapel Road. I suppose one could not have described it as being architecturally attractive, but it was certainly impressive, standing like a citadel of peace amidst a bedlam of madness. We drove past the entire length of the hospital, for the College was attached to the side of the main building, with its entrance in Turner Street. We turned the corner and then, as my brother brought the car to a halt, we were there. I looked up at the building, neatly built of red brick and with a multitude of large windows marking its four storeys.

I slid out of the little car and stood on the pavement outside the impressive entrance. Four tall brick pillars supported a large stone balcony. Underneath was a heavy wooden door. I turned the massive handle, pushed the door open and took my first steps into the new era of my life which was about to unfold.

CHAPTER 2
First Impressions

I still had nearly half an hour before I was due to meet the Dean, so I decided I would seek out the College's toilet facilities and make myself sufficiently presentable to meet the great man. After wandering round a multitude of passages, I came upon a likely-looking door which, as I pushed it tentatively open, revealed the haven which I sought. I washed my face and combed my hair, taking meticulous care that each individual strand was in its proper place. I straightened my tie and regarded myself in the mirror, for nothing must be left to chance. I would like to say that I was wearing my best suit, but it was, indeed, my only suit. Nevertheless, as I studied my mirror image, I was reasonably pleased with what I saw.

It was while I was engaged in this brief moment of self-admiration that I suddenly realised that another person had entered the cloak-room. I turned in the direction of the newcomer, who had advanced to the washbasin next to mine, and I must confess that I was slightly puzzled by what I saw. I assumed he must be a student, for this was the students' washroom and presumably the staff had their own facilities. To me, however, he did not fit the image which my mind regarded as being that of a budding doctor. To begin with, there was his clothing. His pullover, with its polo neck flopping loosely round his neck, hung limply from his upper body. It was of a dirty yellow colour, liberally adorned with holes and with the distinct appearance of having been stretched far beyond the limits which might be expected of the wool from which it had been made. His once-grey flannel trousers hung in similar shapeless fashion about his nether regions, with the turn-ups lying forlornly over the insteps of his shoes. It was those shoes which completed the ensemble and, at the same time, explained why his entry into the room had been achieved without my hearing him. They were the scruffiest pair of plimsolls I had ever seen. I imagined they had originally been white in colour, but that had obviously been long ago. Furthermore, both of them had also acquired a hole in the end, from each of which a large toe extended out into the open air.

As if his sartorial condition was not enough to puzzle me as regards his status, my feeling of wonderment was increased by his age, for he appeared to be at least in his mid-thirties. To me, still a teenager, this man was far too old to be a student. It was while I was frantically trying to unravel the mystery of this strange newcomer that he made the first approach.

"New student?" he asked.

"Hopefully, yes", I replied. "I've an interview with the Dean at eleven."

"Was your father a Londoner?" he queried.

"No", I said. "He's a journalist. But my brother was here a few years back."

"You're alright then", he said. "You'll be in."

"Really?"

"No doubt about it", he said. "If you're related to an old Londoner he'll grab you with open arms."

I was by no means sure whether that statement was based on fact or whether he was just trying to give me confidence. I had no time to dwell on the matter, however, for he continued firing questions at me like short, sharp bursts of machine gun fire.

"Play rugger?„

"No", I said. "I'm afraid not."

"Pity", he said. "Never mind. Can't be helped. Play anything else?"

"Oh, yes", I replied with enthusiasm. "Quite a bit of soccer".

"That's good", he said. "The round-ball lot will be pleased. Haven't been doing too well just lately. They can do with a bit of new talent."

He spoke as if I had already been accepted, but I still lacked his certainty concerning my situation. Even so, he seemed to know what he was talking about.

"How long have you been at the London?" I asked. "What year are you in?"

"I've been here nearly six years", he said. "I'm in my third year."

This had me completely puzzled. If he had been there six years, how could he still be in his third year? My look of wonderment must have communicated itself to him, for he immediately provided the answer.

"It's all a question of passing exams", he said. "I came here for the rugger – been in the first fifteen ever since my first term".

"Don't you want to be a doctor?" I asked in all my innocence.

"Oh yes", he said. "But rugger came first. That's why I kept ploughing exams. But Father doesn't mind too much. He was in the fifteen when he was here. He's not too worried. Knows I'll get there in the end."

I was just trying to digest the facts of his situation when, with a wave of his arm, he took off towards the door.

"Must dash", he said. "Got a lecture at eleven."

Then he was gone and I was left wondering what kind of man it was who could take life so casually and yet still know that he would "get there in the end". Our paths were destined to cross on many occasions during the ensuing years and I am happy to report that he really did make it through his finals. When I later congratulated him on his success, he tried to convince me that it was all a mistake. By then, however, I had developed the ability to see through his outer facade of devil-may-care abandon and I knew the truth. It was no mistake. Rugby had eventually taken second place to Medicine. As I stood alone in that spartan washroom, however, I could only wonder as to the nature of the men with whom I was to share the next few years of my life.

Anyway, I decided it was time to make my way to the Dean's office. A porter directed me up the wide staircase and along a passage to the right, and there I found myself outside a door bearing the simple inscription "DEAN". I took a last brief look at the little booklet in my hand, the "Students' Guide to the L.H.M.C.", which I had received when I had first applied for admission. I wanted to reassure myself that I remembered his name, just in case I needed it. "Archibald E. Clark-Kennedy", I read, followed by a long list of qualifications, honours and appointments which seemed to increase in length each time I scanned through them. In any case, my mind was hardly in a fit state to assimilate it all, for it was full of other things.

What manner of man would he turn out to be? What sort of questions would he be likely to ask? What if he simply asked me why I wanted to be a dentist? That would be the most difficult one to answer. I couldn't simply say "Because my brother is one" or, more honestly, "Because that's what my parents want me to be". Anyway, it was too late now to try and invent some sort of clever answer which might impress him. There could be no second thoughts. I braced myself and gave the door the gentlest of taps.

Almost immediately, the door opened to reveal a little man with wispy grey hair and steel-rimmed spectacles. This was certainly not

16

what I had expected, for he appeared to have neither the physical presence nor the air of authority which I imagined the Dean of such an establishment to possess.

"Yes?" he enquired.

"My name is Bagshaw, sir", I said. "I have an appointment at eleven."

He ushered me into the little room and, pointing to a hard-backed, leather-upholstered chair, invited me to sit down.

"Thank you, sir", I said as I gently deposited my nether regions on the shiny surface of the seat. I was trying desperately to display an air of casual nonchalance which was the very antithesis of what I was actually experiencing.

"There's no need for all that "sir" treatment", he said. "I'm just the secretary", and, with that, he opened a folder and began inspecting its contents. I glanced around the room, which gave the appearance of having remained undisturbed for generations. Pictures of ancient medical men adorned the walls, and a long shelf carried piles of professional journals and other books and papers.

"I see you've got your Pre-Medical out of the way", he said.

"Yes", I replied. "Chemistry and Physics in March and Biology last month".

There was no need for me to give that information for he had it all before him, but I felt I had to say something.

"You've got some good references here too", he said. "Now, the main thing is – can your people afford the fees?"

"Yes", I replied, with a degree of certainty which would have surprised my parents.

"Then there's things like books and board and lodgings", he went on. "Can they run to that?"

These questions were of the greatest significance, for there were no grants or any kind of financial assistance available to dental students at that time. I dare not give even the slightest hint that there might be any degree of difficulty in coming up with the necessary cash.

"Yes, certainly", I said, in a tone which I hoped carried the necessary air of conviction.

"Well, that seems to cover everything", he said, "except for the photograph".

"Photograph?" I said. Nobody had said anything about a photograph.

"Yes. We always like to have a picture of every new student.

Nothing special – just postcard size will do. We've got quite a collection in the cupboard. We call it our Rogues' Gallery."

Then, for the first time in our interview, a smile spread across his face. He obviously said this to every prospective student and it was probably the part he most enjoyed. I had no wish to disappoint him and, with a great effort, I gave a little chuckle and forced my lips into the sort of formation which I hoped would suggest to him that I found his remark highly amusing.

It was at that moment that another man strode into the room and I was totally taken aback both by his mode of entry and by his physique. I had never seen such a tall man in all my life, and the fact that he was also of extremely slim build merely served to give the impression of even greater height. His legs were so long that it seemed that a mere two or three strides would be sufficient to take him from one side of the room to the other. Furthermore, as he came through the doorway, he found it necessary to bend almost double in order to avoid sharp contact with the fabric of the building. The secretary sprang to his feet and I did likewise, for this was, indeed, the Dean.

"Good morning, sir", said the secretary. "This is Mr. Bagshaw. He's joining the Dental School next term."

The Dean looked down at me. Then, extending his hand, he said, "Good morning, Mr. Bagshaw. Welcome to the London."

I returned his handshake and said, "Thank you, sir". With that, he turned and disappeared through another door into his inner office. Throughout all the years of my connection with the London, that was destined to be the one and only personal conversation I ever had with the great man. Nevertheless, it was a conversation which completely transformed my life. In the first place, he had called me Mr. Bagshaw – I had never expected to be addressed as Mister by Archie Clark-Kennedy. Secondly, and even more significantly, it had become apparent that I had been accepted as a student. I was on my way.

I left the Dean's office with a feeling of excitement running through my body. At that moment I was oblivious to the hazards and problems which were waiting for me in the coming years. I had gained acceptance and I was in a state of heady euphoria. I almost floated down the stairs to the main hall of the College and then I found myself at the open door looking out onto Turner Street. The air over the East End of London was never very salubrious, even at the best of times, but at that moment I breathed it in with as much pleasure as if it had been attar of roses.

I looked across the road to the outpatients' department where, every day, vast sections of the local populace presented themselves before being despatched to various parts of the hospital for the relief of their multiplicity of maladies. Then, as my eyes wandered

The London Hospital in 1760, surrounded by what were then the green fields of Whitechapel.

The Hospital in 1939, standing like a citadel of peace amidst a bedlam of madness.

around, they lit upon a building with a large sign which proclaimed it to be the Dental Department. I had time to spare, so why not stroll across and have a look around? Why not, indeed? Before I knew what was happening, I was across the road, through the door and introducing myself to Sister Dental.

If the popular image of a nursing sister is that of a fiery dragon breathing flames through her nostrils and ruling her charges with a rod of iron, I can only say that this Sister did not come from that mould. Sister Tennant (for that was her real name, although Sisters were normally known by the name of their ward or department) exhibited a subtle blend of efficiency and pleasing friendliness. Furthermore, she had an obvious pride in her department which became readily apparent as she took me on a guided tour.

Down the long corridor we went, flanked on either side by wooden benches on which sat a varied selection of the local populace, all waiting their turn to submit themselves to the mercy of either operating staff or students. On one side was a continuing succession of doors bearing such inscriptions as Examination Room, X-Ray Room, Anaesthetic Room and Recovery Room. Each door was opened by Sister so that I could peep inside and see what mysteries were hidden within. Then we came to the Conservation Room. This was the part of the department where most of the treatment was carried out, for, as its name implied, it was devoted to the various forms of conservative treatment such as fillings, scalings and the provision of such things as crowns and bridges.

The whole place was a hive of activity and I was immediately struck by the vastness of the room, although I was later to discover that it was, in fact, smaller than those in most of the other teaching hospitals. Along the entire length of the room ran two long rows of dental chairs, in each of which a patient was being subjected to the dubious skills of potential dental surgeons. Various other people were engaged in other activities, some actively participating whilst others appeared to be mere spectators.

It was not long before I learned to differentiate between the different grades of people who were taking part in this real-life drama. The earnest young men in their short, well-starched white jackets were the students. The more casual-looking members of the cast, much fewer in number and clad in long, floppy gowns tied around the waist with lengths of cotton bandage, were the housemen and dressers. Then there were just two or three, older and more venerable in appearance and wearing full-length white coats and an air of authority, and these were the Chiefs. These were the men responsible for ensuring that the students acquired the necessary degree of both knowledge and professional skill before they were let loose upon an unsuspecting public.

There was one other man, standing by the wall in conversation with one of the housemen. He was wearing no protective garment of any kind, so I was unable to determine his position in the hierarchy of the department. My ignorance in this respect, however, was soon dispelled as Sister tapped me on the shoulder and said, "Come and meet Mr. Sprawson". Everything then became clear to me, for he was, in fact, Professor Evelyn C. Sprawson, Dental Sub-Dean of the College and Director of Dental Studies. I had heard much about him, for he was one of the leading authorities in the world of dentistry. His text-books and professional papers were highly regarded as authoritative works and his lectures to learned societies always drew large audiences.

I suppose my face at that moment may possibly have carried a slight expression of hesitation, for Sister was quick to add, "You'll find him very approachable". That description proved to be very much of an understatement for, right from that very first meeting, he radiated a warmth which I was to experience whenever I was in his presence. My initial feeling of awesome respect for the man was destined to develop into something approaching love, for he was, indeed, a father figure. Lecturer and demonstrator he may well have been, but he was also a combination of confidant, father confessor and wet-nurse. Whenever any of us needed help, advice or encouragement, "Spraw" was always available and willing to give whatever time the situation demanded.

One of the first things which struck me at that first meeting was that he had a slight speech impediment. It was in the form of a stammer which, every now and again, caused him to stumble over certain words. I must confess that I found it rather endearing although it caused him intense annoyance. I was to hear it quite frequently during the next few years, particularly when he gave us lectures. Strangely enough, however, I once attended one of his lectures at the Royal Society of Medicine, when his listeners comprised many of the most learned members of the profession, and he sailed merrily through an hour and a half without the slightest hesitation. It must have been some strange effect which we students had upon him!

I cannot recall the details of our conversation on that first meeting, but I know I felt a glow of pleasure when, eventually, he shook my hand and wished me well. I made my way along the corridor, down the stairs and out into Turner Street. It had been quite a day.

My head was full of excited satisfaction as I wandered slowly along towards Whitechapel Road. Then, however, as I watched the bustling activity up and down that unfamiliar street, my emotions became slightly mixed. What did the next four years really hold for me? The East End of London, with its grimy air and unfamiliar people, was far removed from the Norfolk countryside which, until then, had been the only world I knew. Then there was the hospital itself. It was, above all else, a friendly place, but how would I cope with the demands which would be placed upon me? I dismissed all doubts from my mind, however, for I had achieved the purpose of my visit. And, anyway, I had plenty of time to prepare myself. I was not starting until the autumn term and there was a summer holiday to be enjoyed before then. The spring came back into my step and I was at peace with the world.

CHAPTER 3

Prelude To War

As the summer days of 1939 pursued their relentless course, my life proceeded at a pleasant pace and in an atmosphere of mostly unruffled calm. For just a few short months I was freed from the continuous demands of academic study which had been my lot for so many of the preceding years. I was now in the happy position of being able to face each day in a spirit of untroubled relaxation until the time came when I must make my way to the London and start again.

At that stage in my life there was only one disquietening factor which threatened to disrupt the even tenor of our everyday existence. This was the troubled state of Europe where, for so long, war clouds had been gathering. When, the previous year, Germany had annexed Austria, there was much huffing and puffing, but little was done about it. Then, however, had come the dismemberment of Czechoslovakia and, as the whole of Europe made preparations for war, it became patently clear that it was only a matter of time before somebody struck the spark which would set the continent off on a course towards destruction. Britain, having barely recovered from the Great War, was completely unprepared for another struggle of such proportions. Thus, the government strived to remedy the situation, particularly as regards the parlous state of our armed forces. An increase in the strength of the Territorial Army was announced, together with a new scheme under which young men were to be taken from their civilian occupations and given three months of military training in what was known as the "militia". It was the institution of this new force which was to make the greatest impact on our family life, for my third brother, Peter, was one of the first to go. Dragged from his journalistic activities with the *Eastern Daily Press*, he was whisked away to a tented camp in the depths of the Shropshire countryside, where he was to be transformed into a soldier.

My mother did not take kindly to this development, for she had not raised four sons to serve as cannon fodder in somebody else's war. She knew that she could do nothing to prevent it, but at least

23

she was determined to make life as easy as possible for him while he was there. She worked on all sorts of ideas, the most startling of which was the suggestion that we should acquire a caravan, tow it to Shropshire and provide a resting place where Peter could spend his off-duty hours.

Rather surprisingly, my father thought this was a first-class idea. The only difficulty appeared to be in getting the caravan towed all that distance, but again he had no doubts. It would be no problem at all. He would do it! It was at this point that the rest of us began to harbour certain doubts about the wisdom of the proposed scheme, for we did not share my father's confidence in his ability as a caravan-tower.

The memory of my father is something which I treasure almost as much as anything else in my life. In spite of my respect for him, however, there was one aspect of his life in which I have to admit that he was a complete and utter failure, and that was in his ability to drive a car. His approach to the matter was different from that of any other motorist I have ever encountered and even the simplest of trips with him at the wheel tended to become something of an adventure.

He had done a certain amount of driving in the days of his youth, so he was not entirely without experience. As a young man he had owned a Morgan three-wheeler which was the envy of all his friends, and it has been said that, at one stage, he possessed a de Dion Bouton, which was very much a classic car during the earlier years of the century. His marriage to my mother, however, and then the successive arrival of four sons, meant that he was unable to face up to the cost of such luxuries, and it was not until about 1936 that he renewed direct contact with the world of the motor car.

I will never forget the expression of joy and pride on his face when he announced that he had bought a car, nor the smug satisfaction when he first brought it home and parked it on the road outside our house. It was, in fact, a Clyno, a wonderful old make of car which was built rather than just made. It was, indeed, built to last, a fact amply borne out by the fact that it had already lasted for a good number of years before he eventually acquired it. It was a somewhat solid vehicle, heavily built and offering, for its time, a reasonable degree of comfort. The science of aerodynamics, however, was a thing of the future, and the Clyno could hardly be described as speedy. It is possible that, on a downhill run and with a fairly strong following wind, it might perhaps have touched 45 miles·an hour, though even that was somewhat doubtful.

It had one great asset, however, in that it was a touring model as distinct from a saloon. This meant that it had a canvas hood which, in suitable weather, could be folded back to enable its occupants to make full use of the fresh air. The only snag about this was that, because of the many folding struts and snap fasteners which had to be dealt with, opening or closing the hood was a fairly lengthy procedure. Thus, it was always advisable to ensure that the weather was likely to remain reasonably settled before throwing the vehicle open to the elements.

There can be no denying that a ride through the Norfolk countryside with the hood folded back was a most pleasurable experience. Sitting in the back of the car, the passenger was in a somewhat elevated position which gave a wonderful view in all directions. This also meant, of course, that passers-by had an equally good view of the interior of the car, and there were times when this could be distinctly embarrassing.

The great weakness in my father's approach to driving was that, irrespective of how many gears a car possessed, there was only one in which he was really interested, and that was top. As soon as he put the car into motion, his ambition was to get into top gear as soon as possible, regardless of whether or not the engine was in a sufficiently prepared state of readiness to accept such a situation. As a result, the engine would pink like a pair of demented castanets and the entire vehicle would shudder and shake as it struggled to keep itself in motion. My father was never deterred, however, and he was always ready to offer verbal encouragement.

"Come on, old girl", he would say. "Keep at it. You can make it."

At this stage it was not uncommon for us to be overtaken by pedal cyclists who would glide past and give us not only sarcastic smiles but, on occasions, forceful advice on how to improve our situation.

There was one epic occasion when my father decided upon a trip into the country which involved crossing the river bridge at Carrow. The hood was down, my mother was in the front passenger seat and I was in my elevated position in the back as we started our hesitant run away from the house. The sun was shining and all was going well until, as we approached the bridge, we found it being raised to enable a large coaster to travel up to the Port of Norwich. My father brought the Clyno to a halt and we had a first class view of the operation until, eventually, the ship was through and the bridge was once again lowered to enable road traffic to continue on its way. By this time, quite a number of cars had come along and pulled in fairly tightly behind us, and this is when disaster struck for, try as he may, my father found it impossible to get the car to start again. All sorts of noises came from the bonnet of the vehicle and even louder ones from behind as the impatient drivers sounded their horns in unison. My father's blood pressure rose and, although I sat behind him, I knew that his face was turning scarlet, for I could see the back of his neck becoming vividly red in colour. He lost his temper and, waving his right arm, shouted at them to come past. They, in their turn, made it clear that such action was impossible because they were so tightly packed behind us. I offered up a silent prayer and just wished there was somewhere I could hide. My mother bent low over her knitting and pretended she wasn't there.

Then, with startling suddenness, the Clyno's engine struggled into life. Immediately there was a crash as my father put the car into gear. It didn't matter which gear it was – any one would do! Then, mercifully, the old Clyno struggled slowly into life and, with the appearance of an intoxicated tortoise, shuddered and staggered across the bridge. From all around us came the sound of cheering voices from the large group of onlookers who had witnessed the incident. I just sat in my elevated vantage point, looking steadily ahead and watching the back of my father's neck gradually revert to its normal colour.

It would have been impossible to tow a caravan behind the old Clyno but fortunately, by the time of our projected trip to Shropshire, my father had disposed of it and had obtained a slightly more modern Rover. This was quite capable of the task but, though my father had no qualms concerning the matter, the rest of the family harboured certain misgivings. Eventually, however, the decision was taken and thus it was that, by mid-August, the caravan was installed in the chosen field in the heart of the Shropshire countryside. There, for the next few weeks, it was to serve as a holiday base for my parents and me and as a refuge for my brother and some of his newly-found colleagues in the militia. It was an ideal situation for both purposes, although it must be admitted that our living conditions were, of necessity, somewhat basic. In particular, there were no sanitary facilities, and this meant that my father and

The little caravan which fulfilled the dual role of holiday home and soldiers' rest

I had to take certain steps to remedy the matter. Our first requirement was to dig a hole at a selected spot well away from the caravan and then, having done this to our mutual satisfaction, we merely had to place over it the portable toilet seat which we had carried with us. The final stage of the operation involved the erection of the canvas covering which would serve to afford users of the facilities the necessary degree of privacy, together with a certain amount of protection from the elements. This structure, a kind of tall, square tent with a marked resemblance to a sentry box, was supported at each corner by a wooden pole. Each of these poles was then kept in place by means of a guy rope firmly pegged into the ground. Having completed the erection of this very necessary structure, my father and I stood back to admire our work. We immediately christened it "The Annexe".

Another slight disadvantage which was to present itself to us came with the sudden realisation that we were not the only occupants of the field. We were, in fact, sharing it with a herd of cows! At first they just stood and regarded us from a far distance but, before long, curiosity got the better of them and they began to advance towards us in massed ranks in order to investigate our activity. Their gradual approach was too much for my mother, who sought refuge inside the caravan. My father, however, was always a man of action and, arming himself with an unopened deck chair, he

27

advanced to meet them. His efforts to drive them off proved completely ineffective, however, for they would not be satisfied until they had carried out a thorough investigation of the intruders who had taken over part of their domain. Eventually, their inquisitive instincts were satisfied and from then onwards, apart from one small incident, we lived together in a spirit of peaceful co-existence.

The incident in question occurred on the first morning after the day of our arrival. I was awakened in the very small hours by the sound of a commotion outside the caravan and, pulling back the little curtain and peering through the window, I saw a sight which almost caused me to collapse with laughter. There, running across the field, was my father, with bare feet and clad only in his pyjamas, but carrying that same unopened deck chair. In front of him and disappearing rapidly into the distance was one of the cows. The main cause of my great amusement however, was that dangling from one of the cow's horns was the annexe which we had so lovingly erected the previous day. My father's efforts to retrieve it were to no avail, and it was only later that we were able to return it to its appointed place. What made matters worse for my father was that, as he made his way back to the caravan, he planted his bare foot firmly into something which the cow had left behind. It was not an auspicious start to the day.

Through the length of our stay in that Shropshire field, I believe my mother would have been content to spend her days pottering around the caravan and her evenings dancing attendance on Peter and his colleagues. For my father, however, the opportunity for exploration of the surrounding countryside was too good to be missed, and he took us on almost daily trips out into the unknown. Some of the places we visited, like Chester and Shrewsbury, were reasonably within our compass, but there were times when my father was inclined to be slightly over-ambitious. My most outstanding memory of such an occasion was the day when, over breakfast, he declared that it was just the right sort of day for what he described as "a trip round North Wales". Now, it must be remembered that this was nearly fifty years ago, and, quite apart from the fact that road conditions were not so good in those days, our old car had never experienced the kind of treatment it was about to receive.

We set off through Chirk and Llangollen and Corwen and then, at a little village tea room, we stopped for refreshment. We had no idea where we were, so my father asked the waitress the name of the village. With a quick twist of her Welsh tongue she answered him with a sound which was quite unintelligible to us.

"I beg your pardon", said my father. "I didn't quite catch that". She repeated her answer and went off to fetch our pot of tea. My father inclined his head towards mine and said, "What did she say?"

"I don't know", I replied. "I think it was Welsh".

We were destined never to know the name of that little village where we partook of our mid-morning refreshment.

We resumed our journey past Betws-y-coed and the Swallow Falls, on to Capel Curig and then to something which was to give us all the shock of our lives. We were suddenly confronted with what the Welsh laughingly call a "pass" in the mountains, but what is in reality a steep hill travelling forever upwards until it disappears round a corner at the top. Seeing this hazard before us, my father gave the car its head and set off as though he was leading the Charge of the Light Brigade. The old Rover took it well for a little while but eventually the strain began to tell and, much against his natural inclination, my father was compelled to change down into a lower gear. Even this helped for only a short distance until, eventually, he had to accept the ignominy of bottom gear. He achieved this with a mighty crash which conjured up visions of masses of little pieces of metal flying madly around in the gearbox. The car struggled forward, its engine groaning in protest as each yard passed by. My mother had stopped knitting and I had given up admiring the view, for there seemed no way we could possibly reach the top. By some magic, however, the old car gradually got up there, and audible sighs could be clearly heard echoing through the mountain air.

It was then that our feeling of relief was suddenly snatched from us, however, for, as we rounded the bend, we realised that we had not yet reached the top. The road continued upwards in a repetition of the stretch which we had just covered, and we knew there was little likelihood of our conquering this challenge. By now, my mother's knitting had fallen from her hands and she hung on grimly, trying not to look at the sheer drop which ran down from the unguarded side of the road. I, for my part, was wondering what would happen if we were compelled to stop and whether the handbrake was good enough to prevent us from retracing our steps in a backward direction down that mountainous slope. My father was oblivious to everything, however, for he was deeply engaged in conversation with his car, offering it his usual verbal encouragement as it struggled forward.

I shall never know how we managed it, but somehow he persuaded the old Rover to inch its way to the very top. There we prevailed upon him to stop for a while so that we could regain our composure. My mother refused to leave the car, but I seized the opportunity to have a relaxing stroll and a welcome breath of fresh air.

Then we were off on the downward run but, even then, the drama was far from finished. My father went bowling along in top gear, using the footbrake to steady our dash down the steep incline. As a result, it was not long before I detected a smell of burning. I mentioned this to my father, but he assured me that everything was under control. Then I stuck my head out of the window and, looking down, I saw flames emerging from the offside wheel.

"Dad", I yelled. "We're on fire!"

Fortunately, he made no delay in bringing the car to a halt and all three of us fell madly out. There was no mistaking the fact that we were now in real trouble. As luck would have it, however, the old Rover was fitted with a fire extinguisher as standard equipment. The big question then was whether or not it would function, for we had never tried it out. I am happy to say that luck was on our side and one good squirt on the affected area brought the situation back to normal. Then we were all back in the car and my father was happily bowling along as though nothing had happened.

By this time, the day was wearing on and we were anxious to get back to Oswestry before dark, for we were on strange roads and the car's lighting system was by no means brilliant. We made our way through Ffestiniog and pressed on towards Bala. It was there that my father had another of his sudden whims for, seeing a signpost to the right indicating "Bala Lake", he thought we ought to take a look. Then, not content with just looking, he decided we would drive completely round the lake. What he did not realise was that, though narrow, Bala Lake is extremely long, and the round trip must have extended over at least fifteen miles. By the time we regained the main road the light was beginning to fade and we still had a fair distance to travel.

He soldiered on, however, and, just as complete darkness took over control of the countryside, we edged our way through the gate, onto the field and came to a halt beside the caravan. My father was a very happy man.

As the days of late August sped by, we enjoyed our brief spell of freedom, with the caravan continuing to serve its dual purpose of holiday home and Soldiers' Rest. All the while, we refused to allow our minds to dwell on events in Europe. This was not difficult, for we rarely saw a newspaper and our little portable wireless set, with its weak and crackling sound, was used only sparingly. In any case, everybody kept saying there would be no war, although the general lack of conviction which accompanied these statements made it plain that most people believed the reverse to be the case. We all knew by this time that war was inevitable; it was just a question of when it was likely to start. My mother clung to a fervent hope that her soldier son might finish his term with the militia and return to civilian life before anything happened. But it was not to be.

On the second day of September, completely without warning and with their training only partially complete, Peter and his colleagues were suddenly whisked away to a military base in Swansea. Then, early on the next day, we learned that the Prime Minister was to broadcast to the nation at 11.15. I think everybody knew what he was about to tell us, but we still hoped we might be wrong. We switched on the wireless and heard the distorted voice coming through to the accompaniment of crackling atmospherics.

"I have to tell you", said the voice, "that we are now at war with Germany".

One might think that such an announcement would have caused a degree of panic or, at least, some feeling of excitement. In fact, however, the effect was just the reverse. The news was such an anti-climax after so long a period of uncertainty that it was received more with a feeling of relief. At last it had come. We now knew where we stood.

Our first task was to hitch up the caravan and get home as soon as possible. Thus, we took our leave of that little Shropshire field and headed back towards Norfolk. It was a long, slow journey which my father accomplished with consummate skill and, by the time we arrived home, darkness had fallen. We manoeuvred both car and caravan into their appointed places in the back yard and then, going indoors, switched on the lights. Almost immediately from outside the house came the raucous sound of a man's voice.

"Put those lights out!" he demanded.

We had been out of touch with any form of communication throughout our journey and we were unaware that a total black-out had been ordered throughout the country. It was my first introduction to the rigours of war. It was, furthermore, the prelude to six years of madness and murder, at the end of which our lives, in common with those of many millions of other people, would never again be the same.

CHAPTER 4

Claybury

Though the outbreak of war was not accompanied by the degree of jingoistic fervour which had existed in 1914, most sections of the community buckled down to the task of remedying the state of unpreparedness which existed throughout the country. It was probably in the matter of civil defence where work went ahead with the most frantic speed, for there was now the ever-present threat of enemy air raids, and it was the fear of such attacks which now brought about a slight change in my future arrangements. I was due to start at the London by the beginning of October and, as the College offered no accommodation for students, I was already turning my mind to the question of finding some digs in the vicinity. It was then that an alteration to my plans was forced upon me.

The London Hospital, with more than 800 beds, still held its place as the largest voluntary hospital in the country. However, situated as it was in the heart of the East End and on the very edge of London's dockland, it would have proved a vulnerable target to German bombers. Thus the decision was taken to reduce it to a mere 200 beds, with others held in reserve for casualties. Staff and students were dispersed across 45 sector hospitals throughout East London and into many parts of Essex, and my own personal situation was that I was required to present myself at Claybury Hospital in Woodford Bridge.

Woodford Bridge was, to me, completely unknown territory, so how could I find digs in such a place? My father had a brainwave. There must be a local clergyman, so why not write to him? It was then that fortune smiled upon me, for the Vicar made enquiries and reported that Mr and Mrs Lovell at Number Sixty Brunel Road would be happy to receive me. They were not in the habit of taking paying guests, but their situation was such that they would welcome the thirty shillings a week which I was required to pay. Thus the decision was taken and arrangements were made for them to take me under their wing.

I had never met the couple, nor had I seen the accommodation which was to be offered to me. That chance enquiry made of the local vicar, however, must surely have been directed by the hand of Fate for, if I had searched the length and breadth of London, I could never have found a more loving and understanding pair of people with whom to spend the next few years of my life.

I presented myself at their door on a Sunday afternoon, the day before I was required to report at Claybury. They were both in the hall to receive me – she buxom and round-faced with a no-nonsense hairstyle and a welcoming smile; he much smaller in build, a dapper little man with a firm handshake and a warm greeting. I suppose many would have described them as old-fashioned. Certainly they had a somewhat Victorian look about them and their attitude to life was based on age-old principles. Intensely patriotic and pro-Royalist, they were also highly intelligent and had obviously known better times. Both, indeed, had earlier held responsible positions on the distribution side of a Fleet Street newspaper. Falling sales, however, had led to the loss of those posts and, while Sybil busied herself with household duties, Ben worked as a store-man at a silk factory in Walthamstow. Though having grudgingly adapted themselves to their changed situation, they still looked back to the better times when they had spent their days in "The City" rather than in the drab mediocrity of featureless suburban streets.

In many ways I found it necessary to adapt my habits to conform with theirs, for I could not expect them to change their way of life purely on my account. The first change came about because of their love of coffee whereas, at home, we had usually preferred tea. Furthermore, they always took their coffee black. Even to this day I have never really been able to come to terms with black coffee. Another early shock came from the fact that, every Sunday without fail, we had salad for tea. It was not the mere fact that it was always salad that caused me such concern, but rather the constitution of the dish for, instead of lettuce, we always had dandelion leaves. Mrs Lovell assured me that they were extremely health-giving, being particularly good for the blood. I found their taste extremely bitter, a fact which I could not help mentioning. She immediately assured me that she gathered them well inside the forest, far away from areas where people were in the habit of walking their dogs! That thought had not actually occurred to me and, thenceforward, I found it even more difficult to eat them with any degree of relish.

My upstairs room, looking out on the little garden, had been

Ben

Sybil

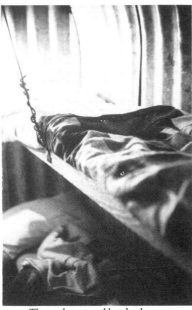

*My entry in the College
"Rogues' Gallery".*

*The underground bunk where
I spent sleepless nights.*

35

thoughtfully prepared for me. A little desk and chair had been added, together with a small armchair, and the open fireplace was already laid and ready to be lit as soon as colder weather arrived. Ben had also been busy making a frame of wood and hardboard which exactly fitted the window frame. Thus I would be able to study into the night without any fear of breaking the blackout regulations.

There was one other feature of the establishment which I had to inspect and, for this, I was led into the garden. There, submerged in a hole in the ground and covered with a thick mound of earth, was the Air Raid Shelter. It was made of corrugated iron and, as I looked inside, I could see that, apart from the wooden bunks, the interior was bounded by nothing more than bare earth. The thought crossed my mind that I would be very dubious about using it even as a tool shed, for fear of rust. Little did I know that I was destined to spend many future hours in that tiny underground dungeon, some of them tossing in fitful sleeplessness and others struggling, by the light of a single candle, to master the intricacies of medicine and dentistry laid out in my textbooks.

I awoke early the next morning and, raising myself up on my elbows, took my first look at my new surroundings. I had slept well in spite of the fact that the bed was somewhat different from that to which I had been accustomed. My mother had always been a great believer in feather beds, which almost enveloped one's body as soon as one laid oneself down. The one on which I had spent my first night, however, was the very antithesis of that. Nevertheless, in spite of its strangeness, it was destined to provide a welcome haven for my weary body on countless nights over the next few years.

I got up and then, having washed and dressed, made my way down the narrow staircase. This was another thing with which I was soon to develop an intimate familiarity. I soon learned, for instance, that it was the third stair which creaked when one put one's foot upon it. Thus, on occasions when I was to arrive back at such a late hour that my hosts were already in bed, I was able to avoid that stair in order not to disturb them from their slumbers.

As I came down on that first morning, I was greeted by the beaming face and motherly attention of Mrs Lovell. A fine breakfast was laid before me and, as I partook of the bacon and egg, she engaged me in an almost non-stop welter of questions and comments.

She was obviously keen on establishing a relationship right from the start. Most importantly, she gave me explicit instructions as to the best route to take to get to Claybury. She had never visited the hospital, but she knew where it was and she assured me that I could walk there in little more than ten minutes.

Her directions were correct in every detail and thus, in due course, I found myself outside the heavy gates which, opening up on to a long drive, carried the inscription "Claybury Hospital". I set off along the drive and suddenly, just as I was perhaps half-way towards the main building, I became aware of padding footsteps hurrying along behind me. I turned round and, sure enough, there was the figure of a young man scuttling along in a manner which suggested that he was late for an urgent appointment. He was a rather strange-looking youth, very slim and with a marked pallor of complexion. He wore steel-rimmed spectacles and, in spite of the mildness of the weather, was almost submerged within a long and rather shabby-looking overcoat. Over his shoulder hung a length of string from which dangled a little cardboard box obviously containing his gas mask. I had no doubt about its contents for a caring government had issued everybody with one of those little pieces of equipment, and I had one just like it. At that moment I had a slight feeling of guilt, for I had not brought mine with me. I had always felt a bit of a fool walking about with that little cardboard box hanging round my neck, and I didn't really think that we were in imminent danger of a gas attack.

I waited until he drew near me and said, "Just arrived?"

"Oh, no", he replied. "I've been here a long time."

Then, without pausing in his stride, he was past me and suddenly, a bit further down the drive, he turned off to one side and disappeared round the back of the building.

I was still considering both his odd appearance and his strange behaviour when I arrived at the main door of the hospital. Then, as I looked up, it all became clear. There, in bold lettering, was the sign which proclaimed it to be Claybury Mental Hospital. Nobody had mentioned the word "Mental", and the idea that I should be starting my training in such an establishment had never occurred to me. Thus, the young man I had mistakenly thought to be a fellow student was, in fact, a patient. Lest the reader should think it odd that I should be thus mistaken, I would hasten to add that, before many weeks had passed, the good people who lived in the vicinity of the hospital were similarly confused. It was not long, in fact, before they were declaring that the only way they could distinguish between patients and students was that the patients always carried their gas masks. As I now look back from a safe distance, I have to admit that there was a certain degree of justification for their feeling of confusion.

As I made my first entry into the front hall at Claybury I was aware of a feeling somewhat akin to that which, in earlier boyhood days, had accompanied each first day at a new school. I had no time to dwell on the matter, however, for there, on the left, was a door bearing the hastily-written inscription "STUDENTS REPORT HERE". I pushed it open and took my first steps into the new era of my life which was about to unfold.

There were a number of young men in the room and others continued to arrive in ones and twos until there were about twenty of us. We were a motley collection, as mixed a bunch as could possibly be imagined. Short and tall, dark and fair, fat and skinny – all were there, and dressed in such a variety of clothing that every kind of supplier, from Savile Row to the local jumble sale, appeared to be represented. I soon discovered that there were eight of us who were just starting. The remainder had reached various stages of training and had been whisked away from Whitechapel to make what they could of these new surroundings in the comparative safety of suburban Essex.

It soon became apparent that facilities for any advanced form of study were sadly lacking. Claybury had a small lecture theatre and one other little room which was offered to us for study purposes. Apart from that, there was just this room in which we found ourselves. There was no library, no museum and, above all, no patients on whom to practise our skills. This latter deficiency was not of immediate significance to me and my fellow newcomers, for no dental student was allowed within striking distance of a living patient for the first year or two of the course. All our early experience was acquired by working with models which, though perhaps giving a visual representation of the real thing, bore no practical similarity to real-life flesh and blood. Nevertheless, we were compelled to satisfy ourselves by making plaster models of patients' mouths and constructing dentures which hopefully would fit unseen gums. This was precisely what I had been doing for the last two years in that little laboratory in Norwich.

We were standing in little groups discussing this and other matters when suddenly the door opened and in came the familiar figure of Professor Sprawson. He had come out from Whitechapel to extend a welcome to his new brood and, no doubt, to try and assess what chance he had of turning us into responsible practitioners. If I say that he was dressed in a somewhat casual manner I am in no way guilty of exaggeration. Rumour had it that he was married to the daughter of a cotton millionaire, but he certainly did not create that impression. Nor did he give the appearance of being one of the topmost figures in our profession. This, in fact, was the real "Spraw", the man who we were all quickly destined to look upon with affection.

We took turns to have a chat with him at a little table in the corner and, as this was done alphabetically, I was the first in line. He was mainly concerned with getting to know each of us by name, but there were two aspects of our conversation which stay firmly in my memory. The first was that, in contrast to our first meeting on the day of my interview, he no longer addressed me as Mister. From now on I was just plain Bagshaw, and this was to remain so until the day I passed my Finals. Only then would the title of Mister be restored to me.

The other feature of the conversation was his ever-present stammer, and it so happened that one of the other new students, Wally Bingham by name, suffered from the same affliction. As luck would have it, Bingham was the one to follow me to the table and, as he tried to tell Spraw his name, he fell into immediate difficulty.

"B--, B--, Bi--," he spluttered.

I couldn't bear to stand by and watch his suffering so, leaning forward, I said, "His name is Bingham, sir."

Spraw smiled and then, looking up at Bingham, said "Isn't it b--, b--, bloody awful!"

Once the formalities were over, we were more or less left to our own devices for the rest of the day. We spent much of the time getting to know each other and spying out the lie of the land. One of the most significant features of student life which revealed itself to us was the existence of what was known as the "book chain". This was a system by means of which text books were handed down to successive generations once the need for them no longer existed. Thus, a student who had successfully passed his examinations in, for example, anatomy and physiology would offer them for sale to another who was then starting the course in these subjects. This might seem, at first glance, to be a perfectly obvious way of doing

Sister Dental   *"Prince Albert"*

things, but what made the book chain so special was that each book had its set price, which was accepted by all and never varied. All the prices had been fixed many years earlier and, by tradition, had remained unchanged over the years. Even if a certain volume was in short supply, the honour and trust associated with the system prevented its owner from trying to cash in on its scarcity value. On that first day I spent six pounds ten shillings on books and was happy in the knowledge that, when I no longer needed them, I would recoup precisely six pounds ten shillings.

The same system applied to the bones of the human skeleton. Here we were more fortunate than our medical colleagues for, while they found it desirable to acquire an entire skeleton, our interest was principally above the neck. Such knowledge as we needed of the main bony structure could be obtained from books or by means of a few hours study of "Prince Albert", the skeleton which stood permanently in the museum back at the London. All we really needed was the skull. Even so there were problems, for skulls were in very short supply and there was, in fact, only one available, with eight of us trying desperately to acquire it. In a commercial situation, the seller could well have offered it to the highest bidder, but that was where fortune smiled upon me, for its owner hailed from a little town in Cambridgeshire. The fact that I was from Norfolk made an immediate impact upon him and it was our mutual East Anglian background which decided that I should be the lucky candidate. Thus, for the princely sum of two pounds, I acquired Yorick, who was to serve me well over the next few years.

CHAPTER 5

The Bore War

As the last few months of 1939 completed their course and gradually gave way to another new year, a kind of uneasy calm settled over the country. It is true that factories were being hurriedly turned over to the making of arms and munitions; it is equally true that, as more and more men were being called into the armed forces, vast numbers of women, going out to work for the first time, were taking their places. Our armies in Europe were being steadily strengthened, a fact of which I was well aware, for my brother Peter had now taken his place out there as a gunner in the Royal Artillery. There was also great activity on the seas around Britain, with heavy losses amongst the merchant shipping which was frantically trying to bring in supplies.

In spite of this, however, a sense of anti-climax still persisted, for the expected enemy onslaught had not come. A single bomb had fallen upon Hoy in the Orkneys on 17th October but, apart from that, the skies above us saw none of the anticipated bomber fleets. It was a period which Winston Churchill later called the Twilight War. To the writers of newspaper headlines it was the Phoney War. To most of us, however, it was simply the Bore War.

To our little group of students at Claybury it was more than just a bore. It was, in fact, a matter of great concern to us that the lack of facilities was holding us back in our studies. Before long our state of unrest had developed into near-mutiny and it was only then that the authorities relented and agreed that, from the beginning of the January term, we could take our rightful place in Whitechapel.

This meant, of course, that I would have to make the nine-mile journey each way, but this did not unduly bother me, for a Number Ten bus passed through Woodford every ten minutes or so. Even at a penny a mile, however, this became a heavy drain on my financial resources so I decided to invest in a secondhand bicycle which, quite apart from the money-saving aspect, also gave me a greater degree of independence. It was that rickety old machine which enabled me to build up a familiarity with the streets of London from the eastern suburbs, through the City and right on to the West

42

End. The bookshops of Tottenham Court road and Soho all came within my range and I can even claim to have circumnavigated Eros on countless occasions as I made my way around Piccadilly Circus.

The main thing, however, was that we were back at the London with all the facilities it had to offer. Not only were we working in an established dental department, but there was also the library, the museum and everything for which we had yearned at Claybury. We had a fairly rigid routine available to us, including regular lectures, not only from our own dental chiefs, but also from a vast array of eminent practitioners in the wider fields of medicine and surgery. Each had his own way of imparting knowledge, some with more success than others, but there was always a varied selection of worthy brains ready and waiting to be picked.

Our lectures took place in a variety of situations. Professor Sprawson liked nothing better than getting a few of us in his office, sitting round a table well laden with microscopes and specimens, and going through his routine without a single reference to any prepared notes. Harold Chapman, also a devotee of informality, took us through the study of orthodontics in the slightly more spacious setting of the dental museum. Many were more formal in their approach, however, and offered us the benefit of their knowledge in a modest lecture room which was somewhat akin to those we had encountered in our earlier educational establishments. Then there was the grandest setting of all – the Bearsted Theatre. This vast arena, with its semi-circular rows of wooden benches laid out rather in the fashion of an ancient Greek amphitheatre, appealed to the histrionic instincts of some of our mentors, for there they could hold court in true theatrical style.

We entered the Bearsted by climbing a long staircase which led ever upwards into an area of almost complete darkness at the back of the theatre. Then, by pushing a door which always seemed to creak when one arrived late, we found ourselves looking down over a seemingly never-ending succession of benches which, at first, put me in mind of one of the stands at a football ground. From that elevated vantage point it was really only possible to look comfortably in one direction, and that was down towards the lecturer's desk. There it stood, centre stage, with a row of blackboards fixed to the wall behind it. The lecturer had his own mode of access into the arena, a small door to one side through which he could, if he so wished, make his dramatic entrance and stand before his admiring audience. This the more flamboyant characters did with great relish, though there were others who were content with a more mundane shuffle into the limelight.

The Bearsted Theatre was, on one occasion, the scene of a most bizarre experience and one which landed me in a situation of acute embarrassment. It was during a course of lectures given by a certain eminent member of the hospital staff who, apart from his many other appointments, held the post of honorary physician to the King. He was a man of immense knowledge but he also tended to be something of a slave to routine. His course always followed the same pattern and during his lectures, which he had obviously repeated over many years, he never allowed anything to divert him from his script.

The lectures which he was giving at the time were always at ten o'clock on Saturday mornings and it was not until we were halfway through the course that we realised that one of them was, in fact, scheduled for Easter Saturday. This was a great disappointment to us all, but particularly to me, for I had been looking forward to the chance of a trip home which the long weekend would have given me. I decided, however, that his lectures were too good to miss and so, some ten minutes or so before the appointed hour, I made my way up that back staircase. None of the others had yet arrived, so I settled myself down in my usual position and spread my papers out in front of me. Then I just waited. The minutes ticked by and still I sat in solitary splendour in the centre of that vast arena.

Then, precisely on the stroke of ten o'clock, the little door down below opened and in came the lecturer. He was one of the less demonstrative types and, without so much as a glance in my direction, he strolled across to the desk. There, donning his half-moon spectacles, he sorted out his papers in readiness for his oration and then, in his usual precise manner, he turned to one of the blackboards and inscribed the single word "Fevers". This was obviously to be his subject for the day. Then he returned to his desk, took a last look at his notes and finally, for the very first time, looked out at his audience. There was a distinctly audible intake of breath as he took in the spectacle of that one lone figure amongst a mass of vacant seats. He looked again, just to make sure, and then, addressing himself to his solitary listener, he said, "Well, you seem to be keen, so we might as well begin".

He placed one hand on each side of the little desk, leaned slightly backwards and then, looking at some vague point in the distance, set off on his oration.

"Some of you", he said, "may remember that, when we last met, we were talking about . . ."

He had already forgotten that he was addressing an audience of just one, and thus he carried on for a full hour, never once deviating from his script and not showing the slightest sign of embarrassment or annoyance. Furthermore, he cast not a single glance in my direction, nor did he, throughout those sixty minutes, give any indication of being aware that he and I were the only two people there.

Then, precisely at 11 o'clock, he gathered together his papers, took his spectacles from his nose and, still looking into the vague distance, said, "Thank you, gentlemen. We will meet at the same time next week." With that, he turned towards the little door and was gone. I had a strange feeling of numb relief. For a few seconds I just sat there. Then, gathering up my papers, I made my way to that squeaky upper door and stumbled through on to the staircase. It had been an uncanny experience.

It should, perhaps, be mentioned that attendance at lectures was not compulsory, although a register was kept and any great degree of absenteeism could bring the offender up before the Dean for an explanation. Some of the more unscrupulous characters found ways of avoiding this problem, and Maurice Hopper was the acknowledged expert. He was always the first one to take his seat, in the back row as near as possible to the door, and there he would sit intently scanning the *Sporting Life*. Once the lecture started and his presence had been registered, he would wait for a suitable opportunity and then slip silently through the door and out in the direction of whatever alternative activity he had in mind.

One or two lecturers, no doubt remembering their own student days, were in the habit of calling the register at the end of their discourse, thus giving late-comers the chance to have their presence recorded. Hopper was well aware of this and on such occasions would silently make his entrance just a few minutes before the end and sit there in a state of fixed concentration which suggested that he had been there all the time.

One other member of our group who had a slight problem concerning lectures was George Webber, but his was of a totally different nature – he found great difficulty in staying awake. He was perpetually tired and he developed the habit of dropping off to sleep in the middle of some learned man's discourse. The first occasion on which it happened came as quite a surprise, for we were not aware of the situation until the lecturer directed a question at him, only to be met with a stony silence. All eyes turned towards Webber, and there he sat, head drooping down on his chest, completely out to the world. As he was immediately in front of me, I made a move to bring him back to consciousness, but I was stopped by the lecturer.

"Don't disturb him", he said. "The poor boy is obviously very tired."

He knew only too well, as we all did, that Webber's permanent state of fatigue certainly did not stem from over-indulgence in academic study. He continued the lecture and Webber never stirred from his slumbers. Then, at the final register call, the lecturer paused as he reached Webber's name and, looking across at me, said, "Just give him a dig in the ribs so that he can answer his name".

I carried out his request and the result was dramatic in the extreme. Webber shot to his feet like a suddenly-released jack-in-the-box and, without a second's hesitation, blurted out, "I'm sorry, sir. I didn't quite catch that. Would you mind repeating the question?" The entire assembly burst into a peal of laughter, with the lecturer deriving as much pleasure from the incident as the rest of us.

Apart from his perpetual lethargy, Webber had one other habit which caused us all a great degree of annoyance. He was forever claiming to be in a state of financial embarrassment and trying to wheedle small loans from us. We were all pretty hard-up and we certainly had no spare cash with which to subsidise his extra-mural activities. In view of his constant claims to be poverty-stricken, it came as something of a surprise when, one day, he invited five of us to a party to celebrate his birthday. He had hired a local place of refreshment near his home in Hampstead, together with caterers to provide the meal. His girlfriend would be there, and he had also invited five other young ladies of his acquaintance to act as partners for the rest of us. It would, he assured us, be "a slap-up do". We marvelled at his unaccustomed generosity and wondered at the source of his newly-acquired affluence. We didn't really relish the thought of a party with Webber, but this was too good a chance to be missed so, at the appointed hour, we made our way to the prescribed assembly point.

It was certainly a wonderful meal, especially in those days of food rationing. There was salmon salad and cold roast beef; there were buttered scones and jam; and there was a mammoth trifle and an iced cake.

"Get stuck in", said Webber. "It's all got to be eaten".

We took him at his word and, before long, every single dish and plate had been emptied. Our female companions retired to some inner sanctum to powder their noses and we sat back to enjoy a quiet cigarette. It was while we were thus engaged that the waitress seized the opportunity to come to the table and present Webber with the bill. He looked at it and then, taking a pencil from his pocket, started to do some mathematical calculations on the table-cloth. We assumed that he was checking the accuracy of the account, but Webber's mind worked in much more devious ways.

"Right", he said. "It's thirty-six pounds fifteen, counting tips. That works out at six pounds two and sixpence each. If you'd like to let me have it now I'll settle up with the caterers."

We were horror-stricken. He expected us to pay for the privilege of attending his party and, as if that was not enough, we were also required to pay for the food consumed by our female companions. We were in a state of mutiny but, just as we were on the verge of lodging a protest, the six young ladies re-emerged and joined us. Everything was going according to Webber's pre-arranged plan. We could not possibly risk appearing mean in front of them so, digging deeply into our pockets, we parted with our cash.

The rest of the evening was to be taken up with a series of games and other diversions which Webber had devised for the occasion, but our hearts were not in it. After about half an hour we made an early departure from the scene with the excuse that we all had a long journey home. Once outside, we discussed the situation in a mood of violent rebellion. Webber had done it yet again. He had put one over on us.

We vowed that, when a suitable occasion arose, we would get our own back. But, of course, we never did!

CHAPTER 6

The Home Front

By May 1940, with Holland having fallen and German armies pushing past Brussels to attack the allied forces, Anthony Eden suggested the formation of a local force to defend the Home Front. The response was immediate and, all over the country, determined men came together armed with shotguns and rifles, clubs and pitchforks to form the Local Defence Volunteers. Later they were given the more inspiring name of Home Guard and were equipped with uniforms and certain basic forms of weaponry. Steadily the force grew in size until eventually it numbered nearly a million and a half men.

The first call had gone out on May 13th. By May 14th Ben Lovell, a veteran of the Great War, had volunteered. He donned his uniform with pride and henceforth, on two nights each week and again on Sunday mornings, he marched smartly up Love Lane and round the corner to the local hostelry which served as their H.Q.

By then I was experiencing a growing feeling that I ought to be offering my services in some form or other. I had little spare time, but I thought there must be something I could do. Thus it was that I became a warden for NARPAC. This organisation, the National Air Raid Precautions for Animals committee, had been set up to provide rescue facilities for animals in the same way that similar services were already provided for human casualties. The first requirement was that we should draw up a complete register of all the domestic animals in the area and, wherever possible, each animal was given a numbered disc in order to assist identification. I was only destined to put my services into tangible use on one occasion in the years that followed. A house on the other side of Woodford had been destroyed in a raid and my register showed that the occupier had kept ten or a dozen pigeons in a loft in his back garden. While the rescue services dealt with human casualties, I investigated the tangle of timber and wire netting which had formerly housed the birds. Then, with help from an interested onlooker, I succeeded in uncovering every single bird, each in a state of shock but otherwise unharmed. I suppose my contribution was somewhat trivial, but I like to think that it did something to help the morale of local pet owners.

As a result of my activities, I came to be known in the district as "The Animal Man", and this unfortunately led to one slightly embarrassing incident. I was called to the house of a lady who had just acquired a new cat. She had been assured that it had "had the operation", but she apparently harboured certain doubts and she wanted reassurance from me that it really had "been done". I had no knowledge whatsoever of such matters and I had no idea what to look for. I tried to make reassuring noises, but I am afraid my reputation was never the same again as far as that lady was concerned.

In due course I felt I ought to be making a bigger contribution to the war effort and I enrolled as an Air Raid Warden at No. 12 Post in Turpin's Lane, Chigwell.

Our accommodation there consisted of two semi-underground chambers covered with several feet of earth and heavily protected by sandbags. The larger one, our Control Centre, was sparsely furnished with a desk, chair and bunk, but it also held the more vital equipment of telephone, log book and a little gadget which would flash to indicate the degree of imminence of an impending air raid. The smaller chamber contained merely a bunk with two blankets and a pillow and was referred to in a rather grand manner as the Rest Room. While the Control Centre was equipped with electric light, the Rest Room had no such luxury. Any activity which could not be performed in complete darkness had perforce to be carried out with the aid of mere candlelight. I was destined to spend many hours studying in that underground haven and, though at first it was rather conducive to eyestrain, I later devised a form of reflector by the cunning use of a sheet of silver paper and this provided me with a comparative flood of light over my books.

As I was rarely able to offer any help during the day, most of my time at the Post was spent in the form of night duty, and it was as a result of this that I came into contact with Bert Pocknell. Bert, a retired jobbing plumber by trade, was one of the two paid wardens who alternated on night duty and it was my good fortune that the rota usually brought the two of us together. I suppose his initial education had been little more than basic, but he was an interesting companion and, even more important, he had a ready understanding of my situation. Knowing of my need to study, he would suggest that, instead of sitting in the Control Room waiting for something to happen, I should take my books and retire to the Rest Room. There, safe in the knowledge that he would call me at the first indication of any impending alert, I was able to spend two or three hours poring over my books until, at around eleven o'clock, I would join him for our ritual cup of cocoa.

This was the part of our nocturnal relationship which gave me the greatest pleasure for, though he was by no means well-versed in academic matters, he had acquired much experience of life and, furthermore, he was a great conversationalist. It was, however, not always what he said which fascinated me but rather the way he said it, for his dissertations were always liberally peppered with spoonerisms, malapropisms and every other peculiarity of speech one could imagine. Thus I would listen enthralled, waiting for the next one to appear. When something pleased him he would say that he was "as happy as a sandbag". Once, when offering criticism of our Senior Warden and the manner in which he organised the running of the Post, he declared, "He has buttered his bread and he must lie on it". He had firm beliefs on matters of religion, although he was not a churchgoer. He failed to see the point of the local vicar standing in the pulpit every Sunday and addressing his flock. "He must know", said Bert, "that he's preaching to the perverted". Thus we engaged in our strange little conversations until, as the clock ticked its way past midnight, I would retire to the other chamber to snatch a few hours sleep before going off duty at six in the morning.

There were two other part-timers with whom I forged a close relationship at No. 12 Post. One was Jack Beckett, a former Barnado boy who, being afflicted with a club foot, was not acceptable to the armed forces, and the other was a local builder named Bartram. We were a somewhat unlikely trio but, between us, we forged a scheme to help to finance the war effort. The government was continually pleading for financial help from the public to meet the spiralling cost of the war. We were all urged to invest in National Savings and, every so often, a specified week would be set aside to raise money for a particular form of weaponry. Thus there was "War Weapons Week" followed by "Warships Week", "Wings for Victory" and "Salute The Soldier". During these weeks, towns and villages all over the country vied with each other to raise the largest sum of money and vast amounts were collected. We three decided that we should play our part and we immediately set to work.

We managed to get hold of a large, circular metal drum with a hole in the middle in which there was room for the three of us to stand. The sides of the drum sloped gradually outwards and, having somehow acquired a large quantity of rubber rings, we stuck these all over the drum and painted a number inside each one. Each ring was just large enough to accommodate a penny and the idea was to encourage people to try and throw coins so that they landed inside the rings. Success in this would mean that the contestant received a prize amounting to the number of pennies indicated by the figure painted in the ring. Having completed the structure, we spent a long time testing the viability of the project to make sure that there would not be too many winners. Only then did we launch it upon the public.

It was an unqualified success right from the start. We proceeded to take it to every fete and carnival in the area and, in the process, we succeeded in raising many hundreds of pounds. This was no mean feat when one remembers that it was all raised in the form of single pennies. We felt a great sense of satisfaction, but there was one occasion which, for me, was to become the highlight of all our money-raising activities.

It was at a fete at Woodford Green and, as the afternoon wore on and things began to quieten down, my two colleagues left our stand in search of liquid refreshment. In their absence I began assessing the takings, counting the pennies out into piles of twelve and converting the result into shillings. The final figure was over

fifty pounds. It was while I was crouched over my financial calculations that I became vaguely aware of a figure approaching the stand
and, thinking it to be a prospective customer, I straightened up to
face him. What I saw caused my heart to miss a beat for there,
standing before me, was the unmistakeable form of Winston
Churchill. I was, to say the least, taken aback for, although we
were in his constituency, we had no inkling of the fact that he would
be putting in an appearance.

"How have you done?" he asked.

"Very well, sir", I replied. "I make it over fifty pounds".

"Well done, lad", he said and then, extending his hand, he grabbed mine and shook it with great vigour. Then he turned and I
watched as he made his way to the next stall. I was in something of
a state of shock for, at that moment, his handshake meant more to
me than all the money we had managed to raise that afternoon.
Even now, more than forty years on, I still imagine I can feel the
firm grasp of that illustrious hand.

During all my service as an air raid warden at Chigwell I cannot
claim that many heavy demands were made on my courage, nor
was I given the opportunity of displaying any great show of heroics
in the face of the enemy. It was all very different from the situation
which lay in wait for me in Whitechapel but, at the moment, that
was all in the future. For the time being, as the sirens sounded and
occasional enemy planes passed overhead, I carried out my patrols,
often in the company of Jack Beckett, and then reported back to
the Control Post.

Occasionally, for reasons best known to himself, a German pilot
would drop the odd bomb here and there, either from sheer boredom or possibly just to see what sort of reaction it would evoke. It
was on one such occasion that a stick of incendiary bombs fell on
Dr Barnado's Children's Home in Woodford Bridge. Beckett and
I were the first ones on the scene and he was an ideal partner, for
that was where he had spent his boyhood years. He knew the layout of the area and, even more importantly, he knew where a
cartload of sand was kept for just such an emergency as the one in
which we found ourselves.

He led me to the spot and we gave the cart an almighty heave.
Unfortunately, it had been standing out in all weathers for some
considerable time and our sudden onslaught promptly caused the
wheels to fall off. There was only one thing to be done – we would

carry it. With a tremendous struggle we lifted it from the ground, and again disaster struck – the bottom fell out, depositing the sand in a heap on the ground. Even then we refused to accept defeat. We found four buckets, filled them with sand and set off carrying one in each hand.

It was then, however, that we suffered our biggest disappointment of the night for, looking around, we could see no fires. There had been six of them when we first arrived, all blazing away quite nicely. While we had been dealing with the sandcart, however, they had all succeeded in burning themselves out. We were not destined to qualify for the George Medal that night! Still, at least we had something to enter up into the report book.

While Ben Lovell and I made our respective contributions to the war effort, Sybil busied herself with the demands of the domestic front. Food rationing had been introduced and, although the original allocation had not been too severe, successive cuts had made the housewife's task steadily more difficult. Sybil, however, went about her task without a grumble and, needless to say, she still found time for her weekly forays into the forest for those infernal dandelion leaves.

She had a great aptitude for making the best of things and she coupled this with a constant readiness to conform to all the advice and exhortation which came in a steady stream from official sources. Thus, at the first sound of the siren, she would insist that all three of us dash for cover in that tiny shelter in the garden. There we were destined to spend many a long night, and this became a great source of frustration to me. They were both avid readers and, by the light of a flickering candle, we would lay on our respective bunks perusing our books. For Ben, on the top bunk opposite me, it was travel and exploration in exotic countries; for Sybil, down below, it was tales of historical romance and intrigue. For me, of course, it was teeth and bones, muscles and nervous systems. Then, promptly at ten o'clock, Sybil would make a mad dash indoors to brew our nightly cups of hot chocolate. Once this had been consumed, it was time to settle down for the night and this, for me, was the worst part of all. I can honestly say that, during all the nights I spent in that underground hideout, never once did I close my eyes in sleep.

There were three reasons for this. To begin with, it was the general conditions which offended me for, hemmed in as we were within those walls of bare soil, we had of necessity to share the accommodation with a myriad of soil creatures which worked actively throughout the night. Then there was the worry in my mind that I had not been able to absorb as much information from my books as I would have done if I had been up in my room. Above all, however, there was the fact that Sybil snored. This bothered Ben not at all, for he had presumably grown accustomed to it and, as soon as his head touched the pillow, he was off into the deep sleep of a child. For me, however, it was the final straw.

I suffered it as long as I could, but eventually I could tolerate it no longer. In the silence of the night, with my companions soundly sleeping, I slipped quietly from my bunk, made my way indoors and sought the sanctuary of my bed. There, within minutes, I fell gently into the soothing comfort of deep, undisturbed sleep.

To say that Mrs Lovell was displeased with me on the following morning would be an understatement. She was, she said, responsible for my well-being and she considered my action to be foolhardy in the extreme. I, for my part, declared that if I was to be killed I would at least prefer to die in comfort. It was the only disagreement we ever had.

I never went down into that underground cavern again. I stuck to my guns and spent my nights tucked up in bed and, furthermore, within a week Sybil and Ben did likewise.

CHAPTER 7
The Practice Fence

By this time I was getting to know more about my fellow students. Thrown together by the force of circumstance, we were an ill-assorted bunch, but soon we were discovering the innermost secrets of each other's personalities and striking up individual friendships.

There was one little group of three who, right from the outset, stood apart from the rest of us, and they were Goldberg, Finsberg and Hopper. They sounded rather like a triumvirate of pawnbrokers, or, possibly, a firm of Jewish solicitors. It was the very fact of their race which led them to remain outside the general circle, for theirs was a totally different lifestyle from ours. It was not that there was any deliberate form of segregation but rather that they went about things in a somewhat different manner. Goldberg, in particular, stood out for, quite apart from being of a somewhat more mature age than the rest of us, he was always impeccably attired in an expensively-cut suit, suede shoes and a different necktie for every day of the week. To us it was obvious that he had private means.

Amongst the others there were Fred Vine who, like me, was following his brother into the profession, and Brian Cooke who, in spite of being a bit of a swot, was always eager to be one of the gang. Then there were the placid Edwards, the continually fatigued Webber and Wally Bingham with his ever-present stammer. The one with whom I was to strike up the strongest bond of friendship, however, was David Simpson, for we soon found that we had much in common. I think we had similar personalities and certainly we shared many interests, even to the extent of a mutual ambition to join the Navy – always assuming that the war wasn't over before we qualified.

Those, then, were the young men with whom I was to spend the next few years of my life. Meeting each morning and parting each night, we spent every day in a mutual search for knowledge. We sat together in lecture theatres, we marvelled together in mutual mystification at all those specimen jars arrayed along the shelves of the museum and, in spare moments, we shared each other's company in the little common room at the end of the corridor.

The notice board in that little room was by no means a strong focal point, for the messages it carried were, for the most part, both formal and mundane. Lecture times were listed there, together with examination dates and similar matters, about which we preferred not to be reminded. For most of the time, therefore, that crude construction of varnished wood and green baize failed to attract even a cursory glance. Just occasionally, however, something new would appear and we would condescend to give it our attention. It was one such notice which caught my eye as we were enjoying one of our brief mid-morning siestas and, rising from my chair, I strolled across and read it aloud to my colleagues. "Fred", it said, "will be in the P.M. Room all this week and invites anatomy students to join him".

I should explain that Fred was one of our top surgeons, an absolute artist with scalpel and suture. Furthermore, coupled with his vast knowledge of human anatomy, he also possessed the gift of being able to impart that knowledge to his students, a rare combination which was not shared by all his colleagues. He was a very homely man, unaffected by his high status, and, knowing only too well that we all referred to him solely by his Christian name, he was happy to use that title on all but the most formal of occasions.

The strange thing about Fred was that, dedicated though he was to both operating and lecturing, he was never happier than when he could disappear for hours at a time down in the basement theatre where he conducted his post-mortem examinations. There, with scalpel and tweezers, saw and chisel, he would be lost to the outside world as he investigated the cause of death of what he called his "people". And always, as he crouched over his work, a lighted cigarette would hang from his lips, billowing its smoke in an upward cloud around his face. As soon as one cigarette was finished another would take its place. The need for this device soon became apparent to anybody who joined him closely in his ministrations to the departed, and many years of this practice had inevitably left their mark upon him, particularly as regards his physical appearance. His bushy moustache, originally silvery-grey, had acquired a distinctly orange presence, while the central part of his face, similarly affected, had given him a complexion which could best be described as two-tone. One could only speculate as to what effect it must have had upon his bronchial system.

The appearance of his invitation on our notice board created much interest and thus it was that a little group of us made our way down the underground passage to the P.M. Room. We were filled with great enthusiasm, for there could be no better way of acquiring an intimate knowledge of human anatomy than by close inspection of the real thing. By the time we reached the door of his room, however, our enthusiasm had begun to show slight signs of waning, and the situation did not improve as we each took a look through the glass panel which separated us from Fred and his people. There he was, crouched over his work and humming to himself while the cigarette smoke gathered above him in an ever-increasing cloud.

We paused outside the door to consider the situation and two of our number, deciding that discretion was the better part of valour, turned on their heels and fled the scene. That left just four of us, none of whom had had any really close contact with death prior to that moment. In the years which followed we were to encounter more than our fair share but, at that time, we were treading an unfamiliar path. We were, however, determined to go ahead and, with a tentative knock on the door, we almost fell into the room.

Fred's welcome to us was purely verbal, for he remained crouched over his work without so much as a glance in our direction.

"So you've come", he said. "Come and have a look at this."

He pointed to the body with a saw which he held in his hand.

"This is his occipital bone. I'm just going to take this bit off."

He was as good as his word but, as he brought his saw into action, it was all too much for Jack Edwards. He slid to the floor with a thud.

"Take that man outside", said Fred. "And, as for the rest of you – if you start feeling seedy, don't hang about. Walk out before we have to carry you out. And if you do happen to pass out, make sure you fall away from me. For God's sake don't fall across the body or you may regret it."

Wally Bingham could take no more. He glided across to the door and was gone. That left just two of us – David Simpson and me. We gritted our teeth and hung on.

Heady scents assailed our nostrils as Fred worked ceaselessly at his task. First he would hum to himself, then he would point out some object of interest, and all the while the cigarette smoke wafted ever upwards. I looked at David and his face was deathly white. I noticed that, for some strange reason, his ears were even whiter than the rest of him. As our eyes met, he shook his head sadly, turned and made for the door.

I was determined to stick it out, for this experience was more valuable than hours of textbook study. The trouble was that every time I looked at the body my head began to swim. The only way I could stop it was by averting my gaze, but then I wouldn't learn anything. I forced myself to look. Then, with alarming suddenness, my body began to sway from side to side. I looked at the door and noted that it was swaying in unison. There was only one thing to do. I slid across the floor, through the door and into the passage outside.

If I had not felt so ill I am sure I would have laughed at the sight which greeted me. There by the wall lay the prostrate figure of Edwards. Seated near his feet was Bingham, staring vacantly into the distance. Near his head sat David Simpson, an unlit cigarette dangling from his trembling fingers. I cannot conceive of any more pathetic sight than our ill-assorted quartet, in whose hands was supposed to rest the future health of the nation. It was a long time before we approached the P.M. Room again.

Although our professional education was in the hands of the College authorities, it was not they who made the final decision as to our suitability for entry into the profession. That little matter was in the hands of the Royal College of Surgeons, for it was to that august body that we would eventually look for our licence to practise. Thus, the Examining Board of the Royal College had drawn up a set of examinations to which we were required to apply ourselves at various stages of our course.

At first glance the formula did not look too demanding, for the examinations were divided simply into Parts I, II and III. Closer inspection, however, revealed that each part was subdivided into different sections which had to be taken at varying stages of one's career. The added fact that most of them were further sub-divided into four parts, namely written, viva voce, clinical and practical suggested to some of us that there might be times when it would be more convenient for us to take up residence in the Examination Hall.

It was to Part I that I was now addressing myself, and it must be admitted that it was not unduly demanding. The subject was The Chemistry of Dental Materials and it was really little more than an advanced form of the chemistry which we had studied in earlier years. I suppose it was the Examining Board's way of dropping us gently into the maelstrom which lay ahead, for it was something

"Setting Up" artificial teeth in the lab.

akin to the practice fence in showjumping. Even so, there were those among us who achieved the seemingly impossible by failing. I was given added confidence by the fact that I had recently won the Class Prize in the subject, for which I had received a magnificent certificate together with the princely sum of three guineas which, like manna from Heaven, had found its way into my coffers.

Though our clinical and practical examinations took place at various hospitals all over London, the written papers were conducted in a building in Bloomsbury between Great Ormond Street Hospital and Russell Square. London is liberally sprinkled with Squares, many of them made famous by an association with something which is attractive to both residents and tourists. Thus, while Trafalgar Square has Nelson and Berkeley Square its nightingale, Queen Square had its Examination Hall. One has to admit, however, that Queen Square has never become much of a tourist attraction.

Certainly it was not viewed in that light by the groups of students who periodically descended upon it to submit to the necessary investigation of their professional knowledge. They came in a multitude of types and from a variety of hospitals, and each had his own method of approach to the forthcoming ordeal. Thus, whilst some sat casually browsing through newspapers, others would frantically pace the corridors, books held in quaking hands, trying desperately to assimilate some last morsel of information which might prove useful. My method was a somewhat ungainly combination of the two.

My main problem was that I had never been very keen on examinations and I invariably got myself into a state of nervous tension before I even started. Then there was the fact that so many of the other candidates appeared to have a vastly greater knowledge of the subject than I possessed. Before I had even finished reading the questions, their fountain pens would be busily engaged applying that knowledge to paper. Then, with seemingly impossible speed, they would have filled every sheet of paper which had been put before them and would be requesting further supplies. Worst of all was the point at which, after two of the three hours allotted to us, a bell would ring and anybody who had completed the task was allowed to depart. There was always a steady flow of departures and, ignoring the fact that it might be merely a reflection of their ignorance of the subject, I was convinced that it indicated their superior knowledge. I was usually caught in mid-sentence when the final bell signalled the end of the proceedings.

There was never any real attempt at cheating in the exams, largely because everybody knew that the authorities were alive to every possible dodge which could have been employed. A single invigilator sat at a desk at the end of the room and he was supported by a group of porters who, spaced out round the walls, looked down upon the wretched victims rather like members of the constabulary in a court of law. Our individual tables were set so far apart that copying from one's neighbour was completely out of the question. Even if he had written his answers in a reasonably legible hand, which in itself was highly unlikely, they would have been impossible to decipher from that distance.

Every other possible temptation was removed at the outset. All books, of course, had to be left outside and such things as rulers were closely scrutinised lest they should carry important facts in some form of cryptic code. Even a simple piece of blotting paper would, for the same reason, be confiscated and replaced with the regulation issue in pristine pink.

The most obvious method of cheating which sometimes offered a degree of temptation to the more devious characters was to secrete one's notes in the students' toilet behind such things as a radiator or some part of the plumbing system. Then, after the exam had been in progress for a suitable length of time, it would merely be a question of obtaining permission to leave the room, having a quick look at the notes and returning with all the relevant facts fresh in one's head. There were just two things which prevented such a scheme from succeeding. Firstly, when permission to visit the toilet was granted it was usually accompanied by the proviso that the candidate must be accompanied by an official. Then there was the fact that, once we had all been admitted, the authorities, being well-versed in all student subterfuges, conducted a thorough search of all likely hiding places and removed any such illegal matter. Thus, if any unscrupulous character managed to effect a lone visit to the toilet, his hopes would be dashed by the discovery that his illicit information had been confiscated.

The examination system had been devised by the authorities merely as a means of investigating a candidate's knowledge and, in their view, it was fair to both sides. There were some among us, however, who could never see it quite like that. They saw it as a challenge to their fighting spirit and thus it became a continuous battle of wits. I could never see it in this light. Much better, I felt, to face up to things and not complicate the issue by putting myself on a war footing.

It was in this frame of mind that I faced, and passed, Part I. I had successfully negotiated the practice fence.

CHAPTER 8
The People's War

As the early months of 1940 gradually gave way to the lengthening days of late Spring and early Summer, the people of London went about their business with little physical interference from the war. An occasional enemy plane would appear, a few bombs would be dropped and there would be the sound of gunfire and explosions. In spite of those incursions, most of the people just got on with their lives and tried to pretend that all was well.

The effects of the war, however, were making themselves felt in other ways than just the physical sense. Above all, the news from the Western Front was so bad that a strong feeling of depression spread throughout the land. The news we received from official sources was carefully selected and meticulously phrased. Thus we would hear that there had been a "strategic withdrawal", then that our forces had "withdrawn in order to take up new positions". We soon learned the hidden meaning behind these bald statements and we knew that they meant just one thing – our armies were being defeated by the superior forces of the enemy. They were retreating towards the Channel ports in the forlorn hope of getting back to this country.

Belgium and Holland, though professing their neutrality, had been overrun and their armies had surrendered. On and on went Hitler's panzer divisions and then, in a sweeping pincer movement, each of the coastal ports was successively lost to the enemy. There remained just one place from which allied troops could be evacuated and brought back to fight again. This was the little port of Dunkirk and its nearby beaches, and it was to this haven that hundreds of thousands of men looked for some hope of survival. My family, in common with so many others, had a special interest in the situation, for somewhere in that seething mass of retreating figures was my brother Peter. We knew nothing of his whereabouts nor of his well-being. We could only wait and hope and pray.

The story of Dunkirk is well-known and remains a miracle of survival. The manner in which the rescue fleet was assembled was not only a masterpiece of naval organisation but equally a glowing example of the manner in which ordinary people were ever ready to rally to the country's call. A spontaneous movement swept the seafaring population of our south and south-eastern shores and everybody who had a boat of any kind, be it steam or sail, rushed to join in. By the time the armada of ships set sail to rescue the beleaguered troops, it numbered the better part of a thousand vessels. There were, of course, destroyers, sloops, corvettes and gunboats from the Navy. There were trawlers and drifters, and tugs from the docks. But there were also hundreds of smaller craft – yachts, fishing craft and pleasure cruisers which, hitherto, had known no other setting than the quietly-flowing waters of the Thames.

It was on May 27th that this unlikely accumulation of vessels set sail on its mission of rescue. The operation continued for nine days and, when the last human cargoes were brought back on June 4th, a total of nearly 350,000 British and allied troops had been landed in England.

It was on June 1st that my parents received that official War Office telegram. I was, of course, in London at the time but, when I later saw the mangled condition of the envelope, I could readily envisage the state of apprehension in my father's mind as he had hastily torn it open. But it was to bring joy to us all. Peter had been wounded, but he had been taken off the beaches of Dunkirk and was in a military hospital in Scotland.

That telegram brought a feeling of relief to us all but, to my mother, mere notification was not sufficient. She would not be satisfied until she had seen for herself. Thus I was called from London to take her to Scotland in an effort to see him. I caught the first train to Norwich, where my mother was eagerly waiting with her little overnight bag already packed. I was allowed a quick cup of tea and then it was back on board another train, this time destined for Edinburgh. There, sleepless and bleary-eyed, we tumbled out on to the platform and mingled with the mass of commuters, some returning home dirty from night shifts in the docks and others, fresh and cheerful, starting a new day. I had a pre-conceived plan in my mind, but I was not at all sure that it would work.

I led my mother to a platform from which trains departed for, amongst other places, Stirling. Once there, we set off through the unfamiliar streets towards the Castle, which I knew to be the home of the Argyll and Sutherland Highlanders. I had decided that we would throw ourselves upon the mercy of those brawny men with their tartan uniforms and unfamiliar accents.

Scottish hospitality being what it is, they proved to be khaki-clad angels of mercy. They ushered us in, gave us facilities for a wash and brush-up and then provided us with a welcome meal. Then, at the very Castle Gate, we were picked up by a khaki-camouflaged military vehicle which whisked us away along country roads to the place where Peter, completely unaware of our impending arrival, lay in his hospital bed. I can only conjecture as to his degree of embarrassment as, in the midst of his wounded colleagues, my mother embraced him and smothered him with kisses. I have a sneaking feeling, however, that there could well have been more than one amongst those men who wished that it could have been his own mother who was thus greeting him.

It was only gradually that we were able to piece together the full story of those last few days. As the Germans advanced, Peter, accompanied by three of his colleagues, was driving the battery water wagon in a desperate effort to reach Dunkirk. Suddenly, out of the clouds came a German dive-bomber splattering machine-gun fire all around them. Peter took frantic evasive action to keep out of the way of the flying missiles but, although he succeeded in that respect, the wagon finished up in a ditch from which it was impossible to extricate it. There was then no option other than to continue on foot, and this the four of them did. Some distance further on they spotted a pair of horses grazing in a field and, thinking that these would provide a better form of transport, they set about catching them. It was then that disaster befell Peter for, in the process, one of the horses reared up and, lunging out with its hind legs, kicked him on the head. He fell to the ground and, to the dismay of his companions, remained motionless. All their efforts to revive him proved to no avail and thus, knowing that delay could ruin what faint chance they had of escape, they had no option but to leave him where he lay and continue on their way.

We will never know how long he lay there but, in due course, he slowly came back to a state of befuddled consciousness. He was by no means fully aware of the situation but, deep within himself, he knew that he had to try and find his way to the coast. The remainder of his story was somewhat vague, though he had a faint recollection of being picked up by a passing truck and eventually reaching Dunkirk. Strangely enough, he arrived back in England in advance of his three colleagues. One of their first actions on reaching

British soil was to contact my parents in order to tell them of Peter's sad fate. Their reaction on learning that he was already back was one of amazement and relief. Later, the four of them were re-united and destined to fight with the Eighth Army in the Western Desert.

After an hour or so by Peter's bedside in that Scottish hospital, my mother declared herself satisfied with the situation and decreed that we might as well go home. She said it so casually that one would have thought it meant merely a short bus ride instead of a long cross-country trek. Anyway, we set off to Stirling, on to Edinburgh and then another night ride back to Norwich. By the time we arrived, I felt that I had seen enough of railway trains to last me for a mighty long time. Nevertheless, after a brief rest I was off again back to London and ready to carry on where I had left off little more than two days before.

The immediate result of the escape from Dunkirk was a transformation in the outlook of the British people. Where there had previously been utter despondency, suddenly there was heady euphoria. Once the first shock of the disaster in Europe had passed, the ordinary folk demonstrated their strange capacity for seeing victory in defeat and, looking upon it as a divine deliverance, they suddenly developed a new faith in themselves and their destiny.

The trouble was that the miracle of Dunkirk had not been achieved without heavy cost. It is true that the greater part of the B.E.F. had been saved, but only by sacrificing all their arms and equipment, except those weapons which they carried home on their shoulders. Of 704 tanks which had earlier gone out to France only 25 came back , and it was the same with every type of weaponry. Britain was ill-prepared for the invasion which, with German forces massing just across the Channel, now seemed imminent.

Hitler issued what he called his "appeal to reason", calling on Britain to admit defeat. Churchill replied with one of his rallying speeches. We would fight on, he said, "if necessary for years; if necessary, alone". The people responded to the clarion call and, waiting for the attack to come, prepared to meet it. We waited for Hitler to send his fleets of bombers, and their arrival was not long delayed. When they came, however, they were not in fleets but just the odd one here and there. Furthermore, it was not bombs which they dropped but leaflets calling upon us to surrender. The immediate response was that people who found them gathered them up and sold them as souvenirs in aid of the Red Cross.

By now it was mid-July and soon we were to witness one of the greatest chapters in the history of the Royal Air Force. The Battle of Britain began over the sea on August 8th and over land just two days later. Much of it took place over the fields of Kent, where the sky was filled with the vibrating hum of engines and the rattle of machine guns. Much of it could be seen from London, and we stood and marvelled as Spitfires and Hurricanes, weaving down from the clouds, took the sting out of the tail of the German Air Force. We watched enthralled and with a spirit of admiration for the brave pilots who were keeping the invaders at bay. I was as much affected by this as anybody, and it was while watching one of those aerial battles that I made one of the most foolhardy decisions of my life. I decided that I would become a fighter pilot! I gave no more thought to the matter and immediately presented myself at the Recruiting Office.

I was interviewed and all went well until we reached the stage of completing the necessary form. Name, age and nationality presented no difficulty, but it was when we reached the question of occupation that the problems arose. The interviewer looked up at me and, picking up the form, tore it up and dropped it into the waste paper basket.

"I'm sorry", he said. "You're in a reserved occupation. You'll have to come back later. You'll be much more use to us when you've qualified·"

It was not until later that day that I realised that my action had not been merely foolhardy but rather one of complete and utter stupidity. If I had been accepted, there would have been little chance that I would ever have been able to resume my studies at a later date. Furthermore, there were three factors which would have handicapped my ambition to be a fighter pilot. Firstly, I had always had a deep and abiding fear of heights; secondly, that fear was accompanied by a similar dislike of confined spaces; and, as if that was not enough, I had, since boyhood, been sufficiently short-sighted to require spectacles. Even if the R.A.F. had accepted me, I somehow think I would have experienced the greatest difficulty in getting off the ground.

As the Summer wore on, we became accustomed to the sporadic visits of enemy planes, together with the accompaniment of gunfire and the sound of explosions as bombs found some sort of target down below. Even so, the heavy and concentrated attacks which we had expected did not materialise and there were times when, on warm, sunny days, the air was filled with a kind of tranquil peace. Saturday, September 7th was one such day. The sun shone and, in suburban gardens, people cut their lawns and took tea on the patio. In the shabby little streets of Stepney and Whitechapel the local folk, in their normal custom, took their chairs out onto the pavement and sat together in quiet conversation.

Then, just after five o'clock, a little rash of black dots appeared in the sky to the east. Gradually those little dots became larger and more numerous and the stark truth became apparent – they were hostile planes moving up-river towards London. Soon there came the heavy thump of explosions, and then great columns of black smoke began to billow into the air, growing up like trees and spreading into a heavy curtain of cloud. It lasted for just one hour, during which time 375 planes, coming over in waves, spread their missiles over the eastern boroughs. It was daylight bombing, so they could select their targets with ease. They dropped their bombs on Woolwich Arsenal, Beckton Gasworks and West Ham Power Station. They scattered them over the docks at Millwall, at Limehouse and at Rotherhithe. They also spread their destruction among the little dockland homes and tenement buildings.

By six o'clock they were gone and the people of the East End could only rub their eyes and stare in disbelief. The docks blazed all along their banks, on both sides of the river, and watchers looking down-river from the central bridges saw the sun's own light grow pale against the crimson glow which spread over the area.

Soon after eight o'clock the raiders were back, guided to their targets by the huge riverside fires which they now stoked up with high explosive and incendiary bombs. This time they stayed much longer and it was not until nearly five in the morning that the droning procession finished. By then they had left behind a trail of destruction and devastation. Even worse, they left a total of four hundred and thirty men, women and children dead and 1,600 seriously injured.

Sunday saw no more daytime raiders but, by half past seven, the procession began again. For nine and a half hours they dropped

The first air attack on the London Docks, 7th September 1940.

The battle against the flames in Eastcheap, September 1940.

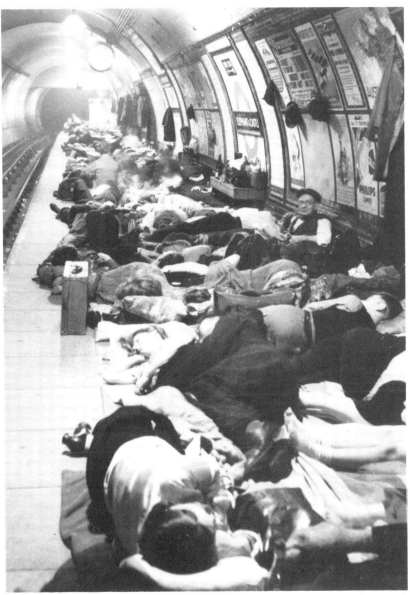

"Nightlife" took on a new meaning as the people of London sought refuge in underground shelters. Elephant and Castle Tube Station, 11th November 1940.

69

their tonnage of destruction and, by the time they left, a further 412 civilians had been killed and 747 seriously injured.

Monday night was the third of the bombardment, and thus it went on through Tuesday, Wednesday, Thursday and so on, right through the remaining nights of September. By then, nearly 6,000 people had been killed and 10,000 badly injured, but this was by no means the end. The nightly raids, with their trail of death and destruction, continued without a break through October and into November. By then, the people of the capital had endured continuous bombing for fifty-seven successive nights. Even then there was little relaxation for during all the long nights of November there were only three when the raiders failed to put in an appearance.

During the first week or two of those nocturnal bombardments I spent my nights at a reasonably safe distance, and it was not until I pedalled through the rubble-strewn streets the next morning that I saw the scenes of devastation. Then, when the call went out for volunteers, I offered my services as a stretcher bearer and, on alternate nights, I would take my place among the vast army of resue workers. As soon as my day at the Hospital had finished I would pop across the road to the A.B.C. for a cup of tea and a bun. Then it was back to the College and into the library for an hour or two of study until the sounding of the alert called us all to duty.

I have searched my mind for the best way of describing my emotions on that first night when I was called into action, and I can only say that I well and truly had the wind up. This feeling soon left me, however, for all around me there were others making feeble jokes and just getting on with the job. I cannot claim that I ever became hardened to the task, but at least I was able to overcome the initial numbness of my mind, for there was little enough time to stop and think.

To chronicle all the incidents of those weeks would be impossible. I well recall, however, one night when, with walls of flame rising from stricken buildings, it was more like sunrise than midnight and it would have been possible to read a newspaper without difficulty. We heard a fluttering noise and, looking up, we saw a flock of pigeons flying round in a never-ending circle. They seemed lost, as if they couldn't understand the unnatural dawn. Above all, they stood out starkly white in the glare, like symbols of peace hovering over the devastation below.

Stretcher bearing by the light of incendiary bombs.
The author is second from the right. 1940.

My over-riding memory of those long nights, however, is of men and women striving together in a selfless, matter-of-fact unity, regardless of the differing backgrounds which had separated them during the day. "Under the bomb", they said, "all men are equal". And it was the bomb which had brought them together. It had, indeed, become "The People's War".

CHAPTER 9

First Blood

Even under normal conditions, social life in a large general hospital is by no means the mixture of mayhem and depravity which fiction writers would have us believe. In a wartime situation it was, to all intents and purposes, non-existent. Even the occasional nurses' dance had been removed from the social calendar and, anyway, fraternisation between students and nurses was frowned upon.

We, in the Dental Department, rarely saw a nurse, and the only times we ever came within smiling distance of the species were on the occasional ward round or when, as dressers in Surgical Out-Patients, we busied ourselves removing ingrowing toenails and smothering our patients with acriflavine. Our medical counter-parts had more opportunities, but even they needed to proceed with caution, for the sight of a student within fifteen paces of a nurse was enough to bring Sister out in a fit of apoplexy with visions of impending rape and depravity. The actual Nurses' Home, known to us all as the Virgins' Bower, was a definite no-go area. We knew it to be heavily fortified, not by means of guard dogs and a security fence, but simply by the presence of Sister herself.

Matron tended to regard all students as lecherous layabouts and she took every possible step to lessen the chances of one of her flock falling prey to their sinful desires. In order to lessen any chance of temptation to the opposite sex, she battled to deprive her charges of any semblance of femininity. Make-up was regarded as a symbol of the harlot, and hair had to be tucked up and tightly encased within that little linen square which, properly folded, became the cap. The only time when any form of social contact was officially permitted was during the annual Christmas Show.

This spectacle, in which students and nurses joined forces, was supposed to be for the entertainment of the patients. With its script flowing over with hospital references and irreverent allusions to senior members of the staff, however, it must surely have taxed the understanding of all but the longest of long-stay patients. Dentals did not normally participate in the Christmas Show, mainly because most of them went home for the festive season. On one occasion, however, we were asked to cooperate and I was prevailed upon to give my widely-acclaimed impersonation of Arthur Askey in a brief (though perhaps not brief enough) excerpt from "Charley's Aunt". George Webber also weighed in with an extremely lengthy, and equally boring, monologue which soon had the audience responding with increasing bouts of coughing and foot-scraping.

In a predominantly masculine fraternity such as ours, it was inevitable that most of our social life should revolve around male pursuits. Thus it was that I became a member of the Hospital football team, with whom I found both relaxation and exercise on Saturday afternoons. It was a particularly talented side, two members having got their blues at Cambridge and another having played for the Corinthians, probably the best amateur team of the day. Above all, however, they were a friendly crowd and, although John Hanworth and I were the only dentals in the eleven, we were immediately drawn into their happy circle. We played against all the other hospitals and also pitted our skills against such as the R.A.F., the Metropolitan Police and various Public Schools.

Football was a very different game in those days. It was a question of skill rather than brute force, a friendly challenge rather than a declaration of all-out war. We always set out determined to win, but we suffered no broken hearts when we lost. Above all, there were none of the continuous displays of histrionic talent which seem to symbolise today's approach to the game. The scorer of a goal did not punch the air and talk of "getting the adrenalin flowing". Nor was he submerged beneath a horde of his team-mates, all anxious to reward him with a hug and a kiss. I was a fairly frequent goal-scorer and the most I ever received was a friendly pat on the back and the sound of John Hanworth's voice from the other side of the field calling "Well done, Baggy!" On occasions when an opponent scored and then proceeded to show what we considered to be an unwarranted degree of bigheadedness over his feat, we had our own way of bringing him down to earth. One of our number would quietly run beside him and, in as sarcastic a tone as possible, mutter, "Mummy WILL be pleased".

We had our own faithful band of supporters who, on a good day, might number as many as eight. It was quite a comfort to us to know that they were on the touchline, and they had their own method of urging us on to greater effort. Not for them such mundane chants as "Up the London" or "Come on You Whites". They,

73

making use of a medical advertising slogan of the day, would give out with a full-throated roar of "Daisy Powders For Headaches". This not only spurred us on, but it also completely mystified our opponents who were inclined to regard it as some kind of tribal incantation.

The only part of those Saturday afternoon encounters which, at first, gave me a feeling of apprehension was the post-match communal bath. I had received a somewhat sheltered upbringing and had not even seen any of my brothers with nothing on since very early childhood. The thought of undressing in front of those ten young men was somewhat lacking in appeal. The idea of joining them as they cavorted in the water and threw bars of carbolic soap from one to the other attracted me even less. However, the situation had to be faced and, before long, the only person for whom I had sympathy was the caretaker who, after our departure, had to remove the large volumes of mud which we had transferred from the playing area into the bath.

I derived much pleasure from those Saturday afternoon football matches, for they were just about the only relaxation I permitted myself. Even on Saturday evenings, having cycled back to my digs, I reckoned to put in a couple of hours study before bedtime. Sunday, however, was a day of peace, usually occupied by letter-writing in the morning, followed by an afternoon walk in the forest and then back with a hearty appetite ready to deal with Sybil's dandelion salad.

It was in September, in the midst of the nightly assaults from German bombers, that I decided to make a start on Part II of the exams. There were three sections to this part, each of which was supposed to be taken in a specified order. I decided, however, that I would attack the third part, for this was Dental Mechanics, in which I had been engaged for two years before I started at the London. Thus, I felt that I could tackle anything they might put before me, and there was the added bonus that, once that exam was out of the way, I would be allowed to get my hands on real live patients. This, with luck, would help me to knock some months off the length of the course.

There was a written paper to be completed, but the vital part was the practical test. It was a bit of a lottery as to what task one would be given, but I was fortunate in that I was required to do a set-up of full upper and lower dentures. This was something which I could almost have done in my sleep, for I had done hundreds of them during those earlier days in that Norwich laboratory. It was probably the only exam I have ever enjoyed. Certainly it was the sole occasion on which I was to experience such a feeling of smug satisfaction as, with my task completed, I looked around at the other candidates struggling to manipulate the assortment of teeth into their appointed places in a tangle of molten wax.

The memory of my first assault on a human patient has stayed with me ever since. To a dental student, the first extraction is one of the major landmarks in his passage through life, rather on a par with passing the 11-plus and stealing the first kiss in one's first boyhood romance.

I had lain awake for some hours on the previous night in worried anticipation of the coming event and, when the appointed time drew near, I approached the extraction room with more than a suggestion of trepidation. I suppose the reader might possibly marvel at what manner of person would be willing to submit himself to the stumbling attentions of such a raw beginner. I must therefore explain that there was no National Health Service and we provided the cheapest form of treatment available. The patient would report to Out-Patients to collect a Treatment Card and was required to pay the sum of sixpence, which would cover any treatment carried out on that visit. The provision of a set of dentures necessitated five visits and thus anybody requiring such appliances got them for a total outlay of half-a-crown. Anything like a filling or extraction which only called for one visit was covered by a single sixpence. There was also the fact that, in those days of voluntary medicine, the East-Enders looked upon the London as "their hospital" and would never dream of going elsewhere. Thus, there was never any shortage of human material on which to practise.

The subject of my attentions on that fateful morning was an absolute jewel. A little Jewish gentleman, he sat in the chair with a beaming smile and an air of utter tranquillity. I inwardly wished that I felt as relaxed as he obviously did. He had been told that this was my first effort, but this bothered him not one bit. Looking up at me he said, "Don't worry about me, sir. I'll be alright. You'll manage it." If only I could have shared his confidence!

The first thing was the injection, and this should have been simplicity itself. It was merely a question of inserting the needle and infiltrating the liquid around the tooth. Anybody who couldn't

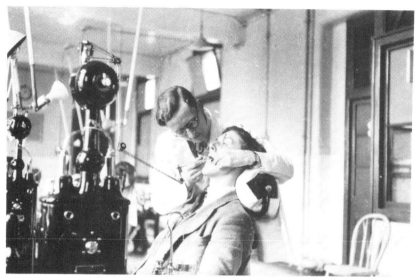

Getting to grips with a real live patient.

manage that should have been shot at dawn. It was my trembling hand which made things difficult, but eventually I managed to control it sufficiently to carry out the operation. Then came the actual extraction. I tried to remember everything I had been taught. "Push up nice and hard", they had said. "Get the feel of the root and don't try to force it." Suddenly, before I knew what was happening, the tooth was out and I was waving the forceps in the air in triumph. There was nothing to it – it was a piece of cake.

The patient had a quick rinse and trotted off, loudly declaring that it had been sixpence well spent. I, for my part, was in a seventh heaven of delight. Extracting a tooth was child's play. It was only later, when I came up against such things as lower molars and inferior dental nerve blocks, that I modified my views.

My first filling was a somewhat different affair, partly because it was of much longer duration, but also for other reasons. All our practice had been carried out on what was called a phantom head. This was a metal contraption which was supposed to represent a human skull, with natural teeth implanted in a base of hard black wax. I suppose it did have some vague similarity to its human counterpart, but it was also lacking in certain vital respects. There was nothing about it to represent the cheeks, nothing in the way of a tongue and, worst of all, it always remained completely

76

immobile, which is something no human patient ever does. Nevertheless, we gradually came to terms with the real thing. From then on it was a question of getting our hands on as many patients as possible. This all took place in the mornings, for everything was supervised by the housemen and chiefs, and they all disappeared at lunchtime. The rest of the day was devoted to lectures and swotting in readiness for the next visit to Queen Square. In my case this was Anatomy and Physiology.

It was at this point that a stranger appeared in our midst in the form of a smartly-dressed man in his mid-fifties, with unfamiliar features and a strange accent. His name was Rudolf Klein and he was a Jewish refugee from Czechoslovakia. He had practised dentistry in his home country but, as his qualification was not recognised by the Royal College of Surgeons, he was required to undergo further study in certain subjects. He immediately encountered difficulties, largely because of his lack of command of the English language, and it was because of this that he sought my help.

He was tackling anatomy and, knowing that I was well into the subject, he asked me if I would give him a course of private tuition. This was something which I would not normally have considered, but there were three considerations which finally swayed me into agreeing. For one thing, I felt rather sorry for him, and then there was the thought that, while teaching him, I would, in effect, be carrying out my own revision course. The factor which finally tipped the scales, however, was that he offered to pay me half-a-crown an hour for my services. Thus, twice a week, I would lead him to my favourite alcove in the library and, for a couple of hours, we would work our way through the mysteries of the human body. The outcome was highly successful for, while he gradually built up a degree of confidence, I completed my revision for the December exam and, in the process, benefitted to the tune of ten shillings a week.

When we finally completed our twice-weekly series of get-togethers, Klein expressed his wish that, in order to show his gratitude, he should take me out for a meal. I was not over-enthusiastic and, when he stressed the fact that it would be "a real Jewish meal", the idea began to have even less appeal. He was insistent, however, and in due course I found myself in a kosher restaurant in Mansell Street in company with a score or so of other diners, all of the Jewish faith. They derived great pleasure from having a gentile in their midst and, while I attempted to apply myself to a meal which I found singularly unattractive, they engaged in a continual banter of jocular comment. Much of it was conducted in their own language, but it was obviously directed at me and I felt a growing feeling of discomfort. I wished there was some way in which I could retaliate but, although I had picked up a few words of Yiddish, I had no idea of their meanings. Eventually, however, my patience became stretched to breaking point and it was then that I recalled a certain word which our Jewish colleagues in the Dental Department often used when we gentiles caused them annoyance. Its actual meaning was unknown to me, but I knew it to be a symbol of anger and dislike. Thus, almost without thinking, I found myself shouting the word at the top of my voice. The result was dramatic in the extreme though somewhat surprising, for the entire gathering fell about in peals of laughter. It was only later that I discovered that the word, very loosely translated into English, meant "You non-Jewish person of doubtful parentage".

With my anatomy exam out of the way it was a matter of preparing for the next one, and all the while the people of London lived their lives against a background of bombing and slaughter. By the end of 1940 the attacks had spread to all parts of the capital and it was then that the great fire raid on the City itself left vast areas around St Paul's and Guildhall enveloped in flames.

The arrival of 1941 saw no relief, and all the while the devastation spread and the casualties mounted. Buckingham Palace was bombed, and the King spoke on the wireless to reassure his people. The Queen made a broadcast specially directed to the women working on the "home front". Even Princess Elizabeth was called in to speak to the evacuee children who had been whisked away from their homes to places of safety.

One personal difficulty which I encountered at that time arose from the fact that drivers of London Transport buses had been instructed, at the first sound of an alert, to divert from their normal route and proceed at full speed on the quickest route to the outskirts of the capital. On an examination day I always travelled by bus rather than by cycle, in order to conserve my energy. Thus, I would alight at High Holborn near the junction with Southampton Row and then have just a short walk to Queen Square, leaving myself a comfortable few minutes before the start of the exam.

It was on one such occasion that, just as the bus was approaching my stopping place, the sirens sounded. The driver put his foot down on the accelerator, swung violently round the corner into Kingsway and set off for Waterloo Bridge – completely in the wrong direction for me. I shouted to the conductress to stop him, but she refused. I frantically rang the bell, but it had no effect. There was only one thing to be done. I braced myself and took a flying leap off the vehicle. I landed in an ungainly heap, slid across the pavement and came to rest against the wall. Apart from grazed knuckles and a somewhat tender skull there was no great damage, but it was hardly an auspicious start to the day.

Such hazards, however, were not destined to continue for too much longer. On May 10th the Luftwaffe broke its record for casualty figures by killing 1,500 civilians and injuring 2,000 more in five moonlit hours. Then the raids gradually eased off until on July 27th, after eleven long and arduous months, the bombers paid their final visit. By then, the Luftwaffe had certainly left much by which the people of London would remember it.

CHAPTER 10
Journey's End

We regarded the approach of our Final Examinations in precisely the same manner as we would have faced death itself. Lest that should sound something of an exaggeration, I would point out that each shared certain inescapable features. Both were unfortunate inevitabilities and, furthermore, one's destination after either event was decided solely by what one had been doing in the period beforehand. Even worse, just as it is difficult to lead such a saintly life that one is assured of one's place in Heaven, so was it impossible, even in four years, to acquire sufficient knowledge to cover every question which our examiners might put before us.

The main problem during those last few weeks was to prevent one's brain being taken over by a feeling of numb inertia, but I think Dr Johnson knew something of our situation. "Depend upon it", he said. "When a man knows he is going to be hanged in a fortnight, it concentrates his mind wonderfully." That was how it was with us. Concentration was the order of the day in order to steer one's mind away from the feeling of blind panic which became steadily more threatening. Comprehensive study was now a thing of the past. The only hope came through intensive cramming sessions, and these went on into the early hours of every morning. Above all, however, it was now largely a question of tactics, and we all threw our weight behind a concentrated plan of campaign.

In the first place, it would have been a great help if we could have found out who our examiners were to be, for they all had their own individual specialities which we could have swotted up beforehand. The trouble was that they came from hospitals all over London and their identity was a closely-guarded secret.

Then, of course, there was the matter of what questions we were likely to be asked. We got hold of copies of the papers which had been set for the previous ten years and went through them in the minutest detail. We tended to ignore all the subjects which had been covered last time but this had a certain element of risk, for there was always the chance that they might slip one in just to catch

80

us. In the end it became something of a lottery and we just hoped for the best.

In a way, our Finals were worse than impending execution for, while the hangman's noose achieves its purpose quite speedily, our ordeal was almost unbearably lengthy. There were four written papers, two oral tests, a clinical and a practical, and the whole thing lasted for a full fortnight. The written papers, though unpleasant, did have one great advantage over the other tests in that there was a certain remoteness about them. One was at a distance from one's examiners and there was no fear of immediate retribution or direct embarrassment if one made a mess of things. With the other parts, however, one was in direct contact with one's inquisitors, and this called for a totally different approach.

In the first place, there was the matter of dress. We considered it advisable to give the impression of being worthy of admission to the profession even if our lack of knowledge indicated otherwise, and thus we all wore suits and clean collars. We wondered about the advisability of wearing a hospital tie but decided against such action lest one of the examiners might harbour some unknown prejudice against our establishment.

The oral examination, officially known as the viva voce, was of comparatively short duration, lasting a mere twenty minutes. As an ordeal, however, it ranked high on the list, for it is amazing how many questions can be fired at one in such a short space of time. In the written papers there was a period of three hours in which to answer five questions. Thus, there was time for consideration before putting pen to paper. In the viva, however, it was all so very different. Question followed question with startling rapidity and any great degree of hesitation over the answer might create the impression of a lack of knowledge.

Before I attended for my first viva I had received a card requesting my attendance at the Examination Hall at a specified time. At first glance it looked rather like an invitation to a Royal Garden Party, but there any similarity ended. It bore, in the right hand corner, the number 74. This was the number by which I was to be known throughout my Finals. Everything was conducted in a spirit of complete anonymity and, even when the results were posted up at the end of the exams, they consisted merely of a string of numbers relating to the successful candidates.

I presented myself at Queen Square and, in due course, my turn arrived.

"Number 74", said the attendant. "You're at Table Two."
I went into the room and made for my appointed place. There were four tables, behind each of which sat two examiners. The tables themselves were heavily laden with a wide variety of treasures. There was a pile of assorted teeth and a wide selection of bones, human and otherwise. There were a number of sealed glass jars, borrowed from some pathology museum, in each of which a piece of unattractive meat floated in pickling spirit. Then there was a row of half a dozen microscopes, each carrying a slide which might require identification. We always knew that a slide would figure among the questions, and I had tried to prepare for it.

It so happened that, a few months earlier, a new Professor had joined the staff at the London. His name was Bertie Miles and he had given me several hours of individual help in the identification of slide specimens, of which he possessed an extensive collection. As I now looked at that row of microscopes, I could only cross my fingers and hope for the best. Suddenly the silence was broken.

"Number?" said my examiner.

"Seventy-four", I said.

"Right, then. What do you know about migraine?"

My heart leapt with joy for, not only had I suffered from the affliction since early boyhood, but I had read every book on the subject and every paper in *The Lancet*. I set off on a detailed answer and he made no attempt to cut short my oration. I went on and on, and he just sat there staring into space. Eventually, he brought me to a halt.

"I think that's enough", he said. "You know, you ought to do a paper on it. You know more about migraine than I do."

I refrained from disclosing the personal nature of my contact with the condition and, looking down at my watch, noticed with satisfaction that I had already used up seven precious minutes. I had little time to savour that fact, however, for a bone suddenly came flying towards me with a request for identification. Identifying bones was a simple matter when we had studied them on the full skeleton of "Prince Albert", for they were all in their appointed places. Seen individually, however, it was not so easy, especially when one was not quite sure which way up it should be. I gave an answer and the next thing was a tooth. This was easy, for it was the molar of a dog. Then came the tricky stuff.

Pushing one of the specimen jars towards me, he said, "What do you reckon that is?" I took the jar and tilted it slightly, just in case the label had been left on the bottom. It was a forlorn hope, of course, and I had further reason to regret my action, for the pickling liquid was very ancient. As I disturbed the jar, the sediment at the bottom flowed up around the specimen in a clotted cloud, giving a pretty fair representation of the glass jars which, as children, we had shaken to give the effect of a snowstorm.

I tentatively suggested it might be a liver. He showed no visible reaction but simply followed with "What do you reckon was wrong with it?" I only knew one disease associated with the liver, so I plunged in with "Cirrhosis, sir?" Again he showed no emotion whatsoever and, pointing to one of the microscopes, he said, "Have a look down there and tell me what you can see". I did as I was told and immediately offered up a prayer of thanks to Bertie Miles. Thanks to him, it was a picture with which I had become familiar.

Eventually my twenty minutes were up and I was released back into the outside world. There I was besieged by candidates who still faced the ordeal, among them David Simpson. "What did he ask you? What bone did you get? What was the slide?" The questions came thick and fast as, still in a state of shock, I felt for my packet of cigarettes.

For my Clinical examination I was required to present myself at Guy's, where a varied selection of dental cases had been assembled for our consideration. We were each allotted two patients and given ten minutes in which to examine them and prepare an assessment. Then we were questioned by two examiners for a further ten minutes on each case. It proved to be my lucky day in more ways than one.

In the first place there were my examiners for, although one was a Guy's man who was unknown to me, the other was our own Harold Chapman who had taught us orthodontics at the London. I had earlier won his Class Prize in the subject and I knew him to be kindly disposed towards me. As if this was not sufficient good fortune, my two patients could not have been more agreeable if I had selected them myself.

The first was a man who had suffered a fracture of the lower jaw, for which he was already wearing a splint. He was a very loquacious man who happily described to me every detail of his condition, together with an account of the treatment he had been given, the progress he was making and the length of time which the surgeon thought would be necessary for complete recovery. When he finally let slip the fact that he was actually being treated in that very hospital I had all the information I needed. I was able to reel it off in great detail and, when the man from Guy's asked for my view of the prognosis of the condition, I had no hesitation in declaring it to be "very good".

The second patient proved to be an even greater gift from the gods, for it turned out to be a young girl of about eleven or twelve whose irregular teeth were being straightened with an orthodontic appliance. I thoroughly enjoyed the ten minutes I spent describing her condition for, as I trotted out all the beliefs which I knew to be dear to Harold Chapman's heart, I could see his face beaming with pleasure at the brilliance being exhibited by one of his own students. That particular day at Guy's was indeed a happy one.

The Practical examination was a totally different situation altogether. It took place at the Royal Dental Hospital, where every chair was occupied by a patient who had expressed willingness to submit to the attentions of some unknown operator. They exhibited a wide variety of dental defects and it was anybody's guess as to what task we would be called upon to perform. We couldn't hope for anything as straightforward as a simple filling; we could only pray that it would be nothing too demanding. My heart sank when I learned that I had to prepare and fit a gold inlay. I had drawn the short straw, but I had no option other than to face up to the situation. I approached my patient, a young lady in her early twenties.

"Good morning", I said in a tone of forced gaiety.

"What's good about it?" came the reply.

"Good?" I said. "It's a beautiful day out there."

"So it may be", she replied, "but it's not beautiful in here. It's alright for you – you're not having your teeth pulled about."

It was obvious that she and I were to be on a war footing right from the outset. I therefore decided to forgo the niceties of a professional relationship and to get on with the job in hand. I prepared the cavity and had it marked by one of the examiners. I inserted the lining and again had it marked. I took the little wax impression and offered that for assessment. Then it was into the laboratory for the tricky part – the transformation from wax pattern to closely-fitting gold inlay.

The casting was done by means of a little piece of equipment

84

known as a swinger. It consisted of a length of chain with a wooden handle at one end and a small metal cup at the other, and we all made our own. I will refrain from divulging the source from which we obtained the chain and its handle. Suffice to say that the College maintenance staff who dealt with matters of plumbing kept a ready supply with which to replace all those which went missing after every new influx of students.

The process of casting involved heating the gold into a molten state and then violently twirling the swinger round and round above one's head in order to drive the metal into the cavity formerly occupied by the wax pattern. Even at the best of times it could be a menace to life and limb for any innocent bystander, and it was our normal practice to ensure that there was nobody else within striking distance when we carried it out. There is, therefore, no need for me to describe my feelings when, as I entered that little room, I found that there were about fifteen of us all wanting to swing at the same time.

The result was utter mayhem. Arms were swinging in all directions, chains were flying hither and thither and, in some cases, candidates were searching on the floor for little morsels of gold which they had lost in the process. I managed to complete the operation without my swinger becoming entangled with any of the others, but I had grave misgivings as to whether I had succeeded in driving the gold accurately into the pattern. When I then inserted it into my patient's tooth I knew that it was by no means perfection. The gap between the inlay and the edge of the cavity was minute – the thickness of a sheet of paper, perhaps – but I felt certain the examiner would spot it. Sure enough, the first thing he did was to stick his probe into that tiny space. My heart sank – but not for long. "That's fine", he said. "Cement it in."

The last part of our Finals, another viva, took place on the morning of the second Friday. Then, at high noon, it was all over. David Simpson and I stumbled out into Queen Square in a state of shock. Two solid weeks of test and interrogation had left us in a condition of complete mental and physical exhaustion. Now, there was nothing we could do but hope and pray. The one consoling thought was that we would not have long to wait, for the results were to be announced just two hours later. A running assessment of each candidate had been carried out throughout the previous two weeks, and this last exam was a mere formality. Precisely at two o'clock the numbers of the successful candidates would be posted up in the little glass case at the side of the Examination Hall. This speedy release of the results had been introduced some years earlier when it was found that a long delay brought with it a sharp increase in the suicide rate. David and I didn't exactly feel suicidal, but we did rather wish that the next two hours would pass rather more quickly.

We decided to go and have some lunch, so we made our way to the A.B.C. in Southampton Row, where we were joined by Jack Edwards. Once there, we realised that we had no appetite for food, so the three of us shared a pot of tea, squeezing every drop of flavour from the leaves by means of frequent replenishments of hot water. After an hour the pot had nothing more to offer us and, as we were beginning to get threatening glances from the waitresses, we decided to move on. We set off with measured tread back along Southampton Row, vainly trying to appear casual and relaxed. Then, as we came to the Post Office, Edwards decided that he would draw some money out of his Savings Bank account so that we could celebrate.

"We may have nothing to celebrate", I reminded him.

"Well, at least we can drown our sorrows", he replied.

It was as we entered the Post Office that we suddenly encountered the familiar figures of Goldberg, Finsberg and Hopper. Seeing us, Goldberg came across and, pointing to each of us in turn, said, "You're through. And you're through. And you're through!" The results had been put up early, and they had seen them. Edwards forgot all about the Savings Bank as the three of us set off in a headlong dash for Queen Square. I had always been something of a sprinter and I was the first to peer into that little glass case with its bare list of numbers. I was struggling for breath and my eyes showed a marked disinclination to focus, but there it was – that magic number 74. David later said that I lifted him bodily up and kissed him in the middle of the street and, though I have no recollection of such an occurrence, I can well believe that it did happen. At that moment anything was possible, for all three of us had passed.

CHAPTER 11
The Licentiate

David and I had shared a long-standing wish to join the Navy and one of the first things we did on getting our results was to set about making it a reality. We decided, furthermore, that we would do it with a certain degree of style. Not for us some pokey little recruiting office in a dingy back street. We would go to the very top – to no less a place than the Admiralty itself. When Edwards heard our plans he thought it was rather a good idea and decided that he would do likewise. Thus it was that the three of us arrived at Queen Anne's Mansions to offer our services to King and Country.

The officer who received us obviously considered that we were just what the Navy had been looking for and, subject to a medical examination, we were offered our commissions. It would, however, be four months before we would be required to join our first ship. It may perhaps seem strange that, in the middle of a long war, there should be such a delay in taking us in, but the Navy were no fools. They knew that, though we were qualified dental surgeons, we were also completely inexperienced. Those four months could be used to rectify the matter. For the fortunate few there would be the chance of a House appointment at one of the hospitals. The remainder would polish up their skills in whatever way they could.

House appointments were by no means numerous and there was always a long list of applicants for any vacancy which came along. David and I, however, were blessed with good fortune when we were selected to fill two vacant posts as House Surgeons at our own hospital. Thus we forsook the short white coats of the student fraternity and donned the long, floppy gowns, tied around the middle with cotton bandage, which indicated our status. It did wonders for our morale and, henceforth, we strode the corridors of the London with an air of confidence previously unknown to us. It has to be admitted, however, that the financial reward for our work was not exactly overwhelming. We were required to attend for six morning sessions per week, each of four hours duration, for which we received the princely sum of two guineas. But that, of course, was not the object of the appointment – it was all a matter of prestige.

Even so, my memory of the first cheque I received stays with me to this day, for I was nearly twenty-two and for the first time in my life I was beginning to pay my way.

One of the special duties attached to my appointment was that of dresser to Arthur G. Allen, who came second only to Professor Sprawson in the hierarchy of the Dental Department. "A.G." was a fine, upstanding man, not really stern by nature but, at the same time, never given to any great outward show of jocularity. He was, above all, a superb operator and I gained much from my close contact with him. Indeed, it was not only experience which I acquired, for there was also the occasional financial spin-off. He frequently admitted patients from his own practice into the Private Ward for such things as the removal of impacted wisdom teeth and at such times he took me on as his assistant. On each occasion I received a fee of two guineas – I was rapidly becoming a wealthy young man!

All patients needing treatment at the London were required in the first instance to present themselves at the main Out-Patients' Department, where they were seen by the duty Houseman. His main function was to form an opinion as to their afflictions and then steer them in the direction of the department most suited to their needs. Thus it was that the patients we received had first been examined by the duty doctor. The fact that he lacked any dental qualification was of no significance, for he was not required to make a detailed diagnosis. That was our responsibility and, in any case, he would not presume to tell us our job. Even when he recognised the nature of a dental condition, he would refrain from giving anything more than a general indication.

To do more than that would not have been in accordance with professional etiquette, and thus the patients we received carried record cards bearing such inscriptions as "swelling left maxilla – please see and advise", followed simply by the houseman's initials. Occasionally the messages would be so cryptic as to give the appearance of being written in some kind of code. Thus we would read such things as "pt c.o. pain L t.m.j. p.s.a.", which, translated into English, meant "Patient complains of pain in left temporomandibular joint. Please see and advise".

I suppose this method of communication was partly designed to keep the patient in the dark about the nature of his condition, for there always seemed to be much secrecy in this respect. With such a vast number of patients passing through, however, speed was of the essence, quite apart from the need to avoid any damage to the niceties of professional conduct.

At the time of my Housemanship a new young Houseman also arrived in Out-Patients. I had seen him about the place during my student days and, although we had never come into close contact, we had developed a mild sort of nodding acquaintanceship. Like me, he was newly-qualified and entering upon his first professional appointment. Unfortunately, however, qualification had gone to his head and he had developed extreme delusions of grandeur. He had no time for the niceties of professional communication for he was now a doctor, a fact which, in his own belief, had suddenly converted him into some sort of superior being.

The first indication we had of his arrival on the scene was when a batch of patients presented their record cards bearing his inscriptions. Not only were they long-winded and unnecessarily detailed, but they were also couched in terms which had been hitherto unheard-of. Gone were the tentative suggestions and requests for advice. In their place came dogmatic statements and instructions. Thus "swelling left maxilla – please see and advise" became: "acute alveolar abscess on upper left six. Severe pustular condition and marked gingivitis. Entire oral cavity in need of prophylactic treatment after extraction of causative tooth . . . and so on". To make matters worse, he was not content merely to initial his diagnosis; instead he gave us the glory of his full, flowing signature. We marvelled that he did not take things to their logical conclusion and append his medical qualifications.

As day succeeded day, we felt a growing feeling of annoyance. We were quite capable of making a diagnosis without the help of a medical counterpart. We didn't like being told what to do. Above all, however, the aspect of the situation which we found hardest to accept was the fact that he was nearly always right!

There was to come a day, however, when all this was to change. Into the Department that morning came a man with a marked swelling on one side of his lower jaw, together with the distinct appearance of being somewhat unwell. I took his record card and read the inscription which, I knew, would reveal all. The patient, I learned, had an acute dental abscess which could only be cured by extraction of the offending tooth. I got the man into my chair and, almost casually, looked to see the extent of the problem before passing him on to one of the students. It was then that my heart suddenly missed a beat, for what I saw before me was not a dental abscess at all. The poor man had mumps!

This, for me, was a moment of sheer bliss. Furthermore, it was an opportunity not to be missed. I could have sent the man straight to the appropriate department for treatment, but I could not resist the temptation to return him to the Houseman in Out-Patients. I took his record card and wrote out my diagnosis. "Dental abscess NEGATIVE", I wrote. "This is a case of acute epidemic parotitis." Then, with a flourish, I added my full signature.

I dearly wished I could have been present when he arrived back in Out-Patients, but I had to content myself with a gloating feeling of satisfaction which was, in fact, shared by my colleagues in the Dental Department. An hour or two later the Houseman and I were to sit within ten feet of each other as we shared our mid-morning coffee break. At one point our eyes met and I felt a strong urge to mutter "Sucks to you" or some similarly penetrating epithet. Not a word passed between us, however. It would not have been in accordance with professional etiquette!

As my House appointment was for morning sessions only, I decided to look around for some purposeful way of occupying my afternoons. My great interest in children's dentistry led me towards what was then known as London County Council to find out whether they had any vacancies in this field. Accordingly, I made one of my rare incursions south of the river to County Hall, that massively attractive building on the South Bank close by Westminster Bridge.

There I met Brigadier Helliwell, the Head of Dental Services for the L.C.C., who assured me that my assistance would be welcomed. He regretted that he could not offer me anything permanent because of my impending entry into the Navy, but he offered me a post on what he called a "peripatetic basis". I had no idea of the meaning of that phrase at the time, but I was soon to be enlightened, just as I was also to appreciate his warning concerning the conditions under which I would be operating. Many of London's buildings which had not been totally destroyed during the bombing were in a somewhat parlous condition, and he made a point of stressing that the situations where I would be holding my clinics were, to quote his own words, "temporary and slightly basic". I soon found this to be something of an under-statement.

In Hackney I found myself working in what had previously been a butcher's shop, a situation which some unkind observers might consider to be somewhat appropriate. Little had been done to the interior since the previous occupant had left, and the walls were covered with a multitude of cold, white tiles, relieved just occasionally by a highly-coloured representation of the head of a sheep, pig or bull.

Down at the Elephant and Castle my setting was a former public house where the still-lingering fragrance of stale beer mingled with the smell of our antiseptics and filled the public bar with a heady aroma which must surely have been unique in both quality and quantity. I operated on one side of the bar while the children waited on the other, and it was here that I hit upon a foolproof system of occupying frightened young minds.

The little boy in my chair was very nervous and fidgety, making my work doubly difficult. In order to distract him, I asked him to hold out his hand, into which I shook a few drops of mercury. I then told him to hold it tight until I needed it for his filling. He immediately clenched his fist, with the obvious result that the liquid metal squeezed between his fingers and was lost on the floor. By this time the remaining children were becoming restive so, explaining what had happened, I persuaded them to get down on the floor and look for the mercury.

I suppose the sight of a dozen or so small children crawling about on the floor of a pub on their hands and knees must have appeared somewhat strange to any unenlightened observer. It certainly puzzled Brigadier Helliwell, who had chosen that precise moment to put in a completely unexpected appearance. The expression on his face suggested that my future career with the L.C.C. was in grave jeopardy, for he gave the appearance of being on the verge of explosion. It was not until I explained the object of the exercise that he began to mellow and then, as a broad grin spread across his face, he declared that it was, in his opinion, "a cunning wheeze".

The degree of success which I was able to achieve in dealing with the younger members of London's teeming population was to lead indirectly to another appointment and one which, though brief, was destined to endow me with a huge degree of what is now known as "job satisfaction". It was at the Queen Elizabeth Hospital for Children in Hackney, where I was appointed Consultant Dental Surgeon. That title may seem a bit high-flown for the professional tenderfoot which I was at that time, but it must be remembered that many of my seniors were engaged in other matters and, anyway, it was only a part-time post.

My salary for the appointment was a mere pittance, amounting to one guinea for each three-hour session. The sheer joy and pleasure which I derived from my visits there, however, were ample recompense for any help which I was able to give to that wonderful establishment. It is true that it was not situated in the most salubrious of neighbourhoods and, furthermore, that it did not enjoy the fame and glamour of the Children's Hospital in Great Ormond Street. Within its walls, however, it radiated a continuous glow of loving care and affection such as I had never before encountered. Every single member of the staff seemed to have been blessed with a saintly combination of patience and dedication which had transformed a place of sickness into a haven of happiness. My visits to the Queen Elizabeth were truly joyous occasions – with one exception.

On the day in question, I was asked to have a look at a very young child who had been brought in by its parents because of a swelling towards the back of its mouth. The medical consultant, a woman with an immense dedication to her charges, was with me when I took my first look and I suggested that it might possibly be an eruption cyst. This was something which occasionally developed when a tooth started finding its way through and it usually resolved itself without any need for outside interference. Then, inserting my finger and feeling the swelling, I began to have doubts, for it was firm in texture and gave no suggestion of containing fluid. I reported this to the doctor and we tried to decide our best course of action. I suggested getting the child across to the London, but she was in favour of more immediate action.

"Could you incise it?" she asked. "Then we can get a better idea of what it is."

I had no choice but to agree and thus an anaesthetist was called and the tiny patient was prepared for my attentions. A nurse held the child in her arms, for we had no chair small enough to safely hold that little body. To say that I was feeling a degree of tension would be to grossly understate the matter for, though I had done this sort of thing for adult patients, I had never dealt with anything as tiny as this. I became aware of beads of perspiration appearing on my forehead as I made the incision. Immediately, I knew the worst.

92

"It's fibrous", I said. "I think it's a tumour. What do you want me to do?"

"Can you take a section?" she replied. "Then we can have a look under the microscope."

I did as she requested and handed her the precious little piece of tissue. I felt a strong sense of relief, for my part in the operation was now over. Inspection in the lab followed, and it was then that our worst fears were realised. It was, indeed, a tumour but, much worse, it was malignant in nature. The little patient was rushed to the London and immediately given every possible treatment, but all to no avail. Within a few short weeks she had succumbed.

During the previous three years I had seen more than my fair share of death on the streets of London and one might have been forgiven for thinking that I would have become slightly hardened to such matters. But it was not so. The thought of that little bundle of life being extinguished without even having a chance to reach its first birthday was something which would have tested the faith of the most ardent believer. It was the one solitary shadow which fell across my otherwise happy association with the Queen Elizabeth.

Some time earlier, whilst taking refreshment in the A.B.C. teashop opposite the London, I had got into conversation with a young woman who, until then, had been a complete stranger to me. That was one pleasing thing which had come about as a result of the bombing. When I had first arrived, I had found London the easiest place in the world in which to be completely and utterly lonely. Now, however, the people were ready to talk to each other without first going through the ritual of a lengthy formal introduction.

Our conversation ranged over various mundane subjects which, amongst other things, included our respective occupations. It was then that we discovered that there was a certain link between us for, whilst I devoted my time to the relief of human suffering, she was engaged in similar work for assorted members of the animal kingdom. She worked, in fact, for the People's Dispensary for Sick Animals, a voluntary organisation which ran a clinic in a shabby little building further along Whitechapel Road. There, in that meagre little sanctuary, free treatment was offered to any pets whose owners were not able to afford the normal vet's fee.

When she learned my occupation, she gave me a rueful smile and said, "Pity you're not a vet". It then transpired that the clinic was receiving a steady stream of dogs suffering from toothache but, sadly, they had nobody who could offer relief in such a situation. Almost daily, it seemed, they would find owners in the waiting room with pets exhibiting every symptom of raging toothache. Usually it was a little old lady who, apart from the dog on her lap, had no other living creature with whom she could share a bond of affection. Thus, all her love was given to her pet, together with the weekly sweet ration to which she was entitled. The result was inevitable – rampant tooth decay and consequent agony for the animal.

At the time of our conversation in that little teashop there had been little I could do other than to express my regret at such a situation. Now, however, I began to wonder whether, in fact, I might be able to do something about it. After all, I could extract a human tooth, so why not that of a dog? My earlier work in dental anatomy had involved study of the teeth of various animals. Thus, I knew the formation of a dog's teeth and the manner in which they were set in the jaw. I decided I would give it a try.

The only problem then appeared to be the question of an anaesthetic. A local injection would not be suitable and the only form of general anaesthesia in which I was experienced was nitrous oxide gas. This, however, involved a certain degree of cooperation from the patient, and things were difficult enough when such cooperation was lacking from human patients. To expect such help from a suffering dog was completely out of the question. I discussed the problem with a medical colleague who had recently qualified and who was hoping to specialise as an anaesthetist.

"Why not try intravenous?" he said. "What's wrong with Evipan or Pentothal?"

I had no answer to this, for I had no knowledge of such things. Fortunately, however, his interest was as great as mine and thus it was that we offered the P.D.S.A. our services. We were received with great enthusiasm by the staff, to whom we represented some sort of specialist team. I have to admit, however, that we did not entirely share their degree of confidence in our skill. For my part, I harboured certain doubts as to my ability to deal with my side of the operation. In the case of my colleague the situation was even more dubious, for intravenous anaesthesia was, at that time, very much in its infancy. Even with human patients it was not easy to determine the dosage necessary to induce the correct depth of anaesthesia for the appropriate length of time. How much more difficult would it be, therefore, to deal with a collection of dogs of

94

different shapes, sizes and breeds? Happily, we more or less mastered the situation and, for the most part, we were able to bring a degree of happiness back into the lives of both the pets and their owners.

There was only one occasion when we experienced an unexpected problem and found the prospect of failure staring us in the face. It involved a little silky-haired dog, a Pomeranian if my memory serves me correctly, which was the devoted soulmate of the sweet little old lady who brought it in. It was rubbing its jaw with its paw in an obvious indication of great pain and, as I took it through to our little operating theatre, I assured the woman that all would soon be well. She gave me a smile, and the look of utter faith and trust on that little old face was reward enough for anything we could do.

Soon the dog was on the table and the injection was given. I waited, forceps in hand. We both waited. Nothing happened.

"That's odd", said my colleague. "That should have put him out. I'd better give him some more."

He repeated the dose and again we waited for the dog to slide into unconsciousness. Again, however, nothing happened and the dog continued rubbing its aching jaw. We were both mystified.

"I can't understand it", said my colleague. "I've given him enough to put out an Alsatian. I daren't risk any more."

Still we waited and, all the while, my mind remembered that little old lady outside and the look of trust which she had given me.

"Couldn't we try just a little bit more?" I said.

"All right", he said. "Be it on your own head", and, with that, he gave it another shot.

Then, with my forceps still in my sweating hand, I prepared myself for my part in the operation. But nothing happened. The dog continued its refusal to give up its state of consciousness. We had now reached crisis point, for we could not possibly consider putting any more of the drug into that little body. There was only one thing to be done. We must admit defeat. I did not relish the thought of returning the suffering animal to its trusting owner and confessing our failure but, somehow or other, I braced myself for the task. I lifted the dog off the table and, leading it by the length of ribbon which was tied to its collar, took it to the door. Then, as I began to open the door, my colleague and I received the shock of our lives. The dog suddenly decided to submit to the effects of the drug and, completely without warning, collapsed in a coma on the floor.

I hastily shut the door, whisked the dog back on the table and extracted the offending tooth. Failure had suddenly become success and we were both filled with a feeling of elation. The only slightly disquietening aspect of the situation was the fact that our patient was somewhat slow in regaining consciousness. This normally happened in a matter of minutes, but the dog was still well away when we both had to leave the clinic after an hour or so. We later learned that it was four hours before the prostrate body showed signs of returning to normal.

When I went back to the clinic the following week, the first sight which greeted me in the waiting room was the same old lady with her little dog on her lap. "Oh, no!" I thought. "Not again." My fears, however, were groundless.

"He's fine", she said. "I just wanted to thank you for what you did last week. Now, I hope you won't be offended, but I noticed you smoke a pipe so I've brought you a little present."

So saying, she thrust into my hand a little packet of tobacco. I looked at it and read the inscription on the wrapper: "Boar's Head Shag". I had heard of it but I had never tried it, for I knew it to be a somewhat strong blend made specially for really hardened smokers and I did not come into that category. Because of the old lady's kindness, however, I felt I must smoke it. The effect was, to say the least, traumatic. I think the kindest thing I can say about Boar's Head Shag is that it is guaranteed to clear the sinuses. Nevertheless, it holds its place in my memory of the P.D.S.A. and of the day when a little Pomeranian frightened me out of my life.

All too soon this period of my life was to come to an end and before long I would be facing a very different routine in strange new surroundings. The change came with the arrival of a buff-coloured envelope. My Lords of the Admiralty had decided that the time had come to play their master card. I was "required to proceed aboard HMS *Drake* at Devonport on 30th July 1943".

96

CHAPTER 12
HMS Drake

HMS *Drake* was not a ship at all. It was the custom of the Navy to give all its units, from sea-going vessels to mere Nissen hut encampments, the name of HMS Something-or-other, for this was the way the Service went about its business. Even when locked to the shore by concrete and bricks, it lived its life as though it was sailing the high seas. Thus HMS *Drake* was, in fact, The Royal Naval Barracks at Devonport. Furthermore, when, on that first day, I walked along that Plymouth street and through the gates, I was not merely entering the barracks – I was "proceeding aboard".

The language of the Service was the first big lesson I had to learn and it looked like being a lengthy one, for they had their own words for everything. Thus, the floor was the deck, the ceiling the deckhead and the walls the bulkheads. Even my little bedroom was my cabin and, to carry it to its logical conclusion, the bed itself was my cot. Furthermore, though officially classified as a dental officer, I was now to be known to all and sundry as "Toothy".

I had travelled down from London in the company of a couple of A.T.S. girls who, on learning that I was just joining the Service, gave me the usual treatment afforded to rookies. They showered me with expressions of pity, consoled me with their considered opinion that "the first six months are the worst" and warned me that I was in for a few shocks. The truth of that last statement was to be made apparent to me immediately I set foot on board HMS *Drake*, though the shocks I received were hardly of the nature which my companions had forecast.

I was met in the entrance hall by a Chief Petty Officer who, after enquiring my name, said, "Oh yes, sir. We've been expecting you. I'll just get somebody to show you to your cabin." Within seconds my escort arrived in the shape of a very young member of the Women's Royal Naval Service.

"Show Surgeon Lieutenant Bagshaw to cabin 147", commanded the C.P.O.

"Aye aye, Chief", said the little Wren.

I bent down to pick up my luggage and it was then that the Service gave me the first of its many surprises. Stretching out his arm to prevent my intended action, the C.P.O. shook his head and then, raising his index finger in admonition, said, "Oh no, sir. Officers don't carry bags." Without hesitation, my young escort lifted my cases and, leading me off along a maze of passages, took me to my appointed resting place. Then, assuring me of her hope that I would be comfortable, she departed. I had noticed, on the right hand sleeve of her jacket, the little blue star enclosing the letters O.S., which I soon discovered marked her out as an officers' steward. She had joined the Service purely for the privilege of waiting on people like me. I found that most odd.

I was even more surprised to be woken up at seven o'clock on the following morning by a tap on the shoulder and the sound of a female voice saying, "Good morning, sir. Your early-morning tea. I hope you slept well." I might, perhaps, add that this treatment was not destined to continue throughout my Naval career. I was being dropped very gently into the shallow end.

For the first week, they sent us back to school. It was not for the study of normal subjects, least of all dentistry, although we did have our first contact with the various forms of paperwork with which we would later be involved. The first thing we had to master was K.R's and A.I's or, to give them their full title, King's Regulations and Admiralty Instructions. These were set out in a document which was, in a sense, the Navy's Bible, for it laid down the code of conduct to which all personnel were expected to conform. Only by acquiring a full knowledge of the document could one expect to live one's life in the way the Navy demanded – "in accordance with the highest traditions of the Service."

The one aspect of this which presented the greatest difficulty was learning how to salute. In my case, it also caused acute embarrassment, for I had only just become acclimatised to being continually addressed as "Sir". It was not easy to come to terms with the fact that all ratings, even seasoned old sea dogs with many years service behind them, were required to afford me this accolade and, indeed, that I was expected to report them to their commanding officer if they failed to do so. It helped little to be told that the salute was not directed at me as a person but rather at the authority represented by the uniform which I wore. It took quite a bit of practice before I could treat the matter with the casual aplomb of a hardened campaigner.

We were fortunate in that our salute was not the vigorous, "longest way up and shortest way down" affair as employed by the Army. Ours was a much more casual affair, being carried out, we were told, "naturally and smartly, but not hurriedly". Above all, in contrast to the other Services, we finished up with the palm of the hand inclined inwards. It had been that way ever since Lady Hamilton had paid a visit to *Victory* on a day when the crew were busy caulking the deck planks. The sight of all those pitch-stained hands held up in salute was an affront to the poor lady's sense of dignity, and thus Nelson decreed that the salute should henceforth be carried out with the palms of the hands averted from public gaze. The Navy has done it that way ever since.

We studied the manual in great detail in order to get it right, and we paid particular heed to the statement that "Officers are to exercise great care in returning salutes with the courtesy they deserve." We derived a degree of amusement from a following paragraph which declared that "When riding a bicycle or driving a motor vehicle, the salute is to be made, subject to the conditions of the traffic permitting, by turning the head smartly towards the officer when passing him". We practised for long periods in front of a mirror, and we tried out our efforts on each other in the privacy of our cabins. Only when we felt confident of success did we venture out onto the streets of Plymouth to put our skills into effect.

Even then, there could be hidden hazards. An experienced seaman had no difficulty in identifying us as new officers, mainly because the shining gold of our cap badges lacked the tarnish which a bit of sea-time would have given them. It was not unknown for such characters to trick us into returning a salute which had never been given. It was done by a sharp raising of the right fore-arm to suggest the start of a saluting operation, followed by its equally sudden return to the side of the body. We, in our eagerness to respond, thus fell into the trap of returning "with courtesy" a nonexistent salute. The rating would pass by, serious-faced but inwardly chuckling, and we would plod on in a state of confusion and disarray.

One of the biggest shocks of our early days in the Service was the revelation that, in conjunction with our dental duties, we were required to double up as Passive Defence Officers. This involved such things as fire-fighting, damage control and a knowledge of which hatches should be closed down in the event of one's ship being damaged in action.

Our course of instruction began peacefully enough with a session of respirator drill. We stood in a circle while our instructor detailed the finer points of the manoeuvre and then we tried, with varying degrees of success, to master the operation. He kept us hard at it for what seemed like an eternity and only when he was reasonably satisfied with the outcome did he allow us to relax. This, however, was where he caught us out for, just as we were enjoying a quiet chat, he would shout, "On respirators". Out would come his stop-watch and he would time us as we struggled to respond to his order with a minimum of delay. I was always the slowest because of the fact that, before I could start, I first had to remove my spectacles. He insisted that we must complete the operation within seven seconds, but he appreciated my personal difficulty. "In the case of Lieutenant Bagshaw", he said, "I'll allow an extra three seconds because of his glasses". I thanked him for his solicitude and expressed the wish that the enemy might be informed of the extra degree of latitude which I was being afforded. In due course, I acquired a pair of steel-rimmed spectacles with unbreakable lenses. This enabled me to speed up the operation considerably and they also came in very useful when playing football.

Another odd feature of our course was the training we received in throwing hand grenades. We had always regarded this as something which the Army engaged in, and we felt it to be a somewhat worrying reflection on the state of the Navy's defences if we were to be expected to resort to such a tactic. Nevertheless, we entered into the spirit of the operation, hurling the missiles in all directions like cricket balls. It was only when we progressed to the use of live grenades that things became slightly frightening. I rapidly became the star performer, a fact which the other members of the group attributed to my earlier skills as a cricketer. Deep within me, however, I knew that to be a false assumption. My skill came purely from a wish for self-preservation and, once a grenade was primed, I was determined to project it to a safe distance as quickly as possible.

In spite of having suffered near-suffocation inside respirators and impending self-extermination with hand grenades, there can be no denying that the most unpleasant part of our course was fire-fighting. It began quite innocuously with an open fire on a bit of waste land. We took it in turns to approach and deal with the matter with a spray of foam, and this was not unduly demanding as long as one managed to stay up-wind of the smoke. With an inside fire, however, it was not much fun.

We were introduced to a gigantic mock-up of a ship's hold, submerged in the ground and having just two small hatches for entry and exit. A vast fire was lit across the complete width of the hold and we were required to go down there, one at a time, and extinguish it. Only when the fire was out could we reach the hatch at the other end and climb back up to the surface. I dearly wished I could be the first to attempt the task, partly because I wanted to get it over, but also because the volume of smoke increased with every successive lighting of the fire. I watched the first four go down in turn, and only two achieved success. The others gave a tug on the lifeline which was provided and were hauled back to safety, only to take their places at the end of the line for another attempt later.

I was fifth in line and, donning my respirator, I climbed down the metal ladder and heard the hatch being shut and fastened behind me. It was even worse down there than I had feared, for I had not anticipated the tremendous heat which met me as I reached the bottom. I gave the matter little thought, however, for I had decided that speed was the great essential and I went into the attack with all the venom of a charging bull. Almost before I knew it, the fire was out, the escape hatch was being opened and I was climbing out to be met by a round of applause from my colleagues. The instructor was lavish in his praise, for it transpired that I had achieved one of the fastest times ever recorded for the operation. I have to admit, however, that my success did not stem from any inherent ability as a firefighter. It was merely my instinct for self-preservation which had saved the day.

By the time we had all completed the task we were in such a state of filth and disarray that we gave the impression of a group of scarecrows who had wandered in from some nearby field. The most seriously affected part of our persons was our hair, for we had all suffered varying degrees of singeing, and the parts which had escaped were matted together with a mixture of ash, smoke and foam. It was obvious that much needed to be done to restore it to its previous pristine condition and we decided that professional help was needed. It was then that I recalled having seen a little barber's shop in a street just outside the Barracks, with a notice in the window proclaiming "NAVY HAIRCUTS RECTIFIED".

Thus, I led my disreputable platoon ashore and we made our way to that little tonsorial haven.

The barber was busy with a client as we trooped into his establishment and he gave us just the quickest of glances as we sat in a row by the wall. Then he looked again and his face fell visibly. "Oh, no!" he said. "Not firefighting week again!"

He was, however, more than ready to carry out the terms displayed on the notice in his window and he set to work with a will. An hour or so later the transformation was complete. We were all shiny and pink like a cluster of newly born babes.

My first spell of duty as Passive Defence Officer turned out to be a night of acute embarrassment, verging on near-disaster. Plymouth had suffered the worst of its air raids before my arrival but there were still frequent alerts whenever enemy planes were known to be active in the neighbourhood. My duty involved being readily available in the event of such an alert and thus I could not stray far from the area of the dockyard. On the night in question there was an E.N.S.A. concert in the Ship's Theatre, so I decided I might as well spend the evening there.

The Theatre was quite a palatial structure with accommodation for an audience of something like two thousand. It was a great source of attraction to the ratings, for it was a place where, in spite of the presence of officers in the two front rows, they could really let their hair down and give vent to their feelings. The only thing they were not allowed to do was to whistle. Whistling was never allowed in the Navy; it was, in fact, one of the most serious crimes of which one could be guilty. In earlier times it had been recognised as a sign of mutiny amongst the crew and tradition decreed that it should continue to be regarded as a court martial offence. Thus, the only whistling sound ever heard on any Naval ship or shore establishment was that of the bosun's pipe.

This meant that the ratings had to find an alternative method of showing their feelings when something caused them displeasure or resentment, and they did this in a most effective manner. They did it simply by coughing – after all, nobody could possibly be court martialled for such a natural act as that. Furthermore, the sound of a large number of male throats being simultaneously cleared can be quite frightening to anybody on the receiving end.

I had first encountered it at an earlier show in that very theatre. It was the custom that artistes appearing in the shows were entertained alternately in one of the messes. Thus, we would have one group in the wardroom, the next would share the petty officers' mess and then it would be the seamen's turn. This all worked well until a certain much-loved and nationally famous female performer objected to the fact that she was expected to share a meal with the ratings. She considered that her personal status demanded something better than that and she insisted on dining in the wardroom.

I suppose it was inevitable that news of her action should spread like wildfire throughout the establishment, but nobody was quite prepared for the outcome. She took her meal with the officers, but later, as she strode out into the middle of that large stage, her audience were ready for her. It started with a single cough somewhere in the distance. Then came a few more at various points amongst the assembly. Then, within seconds, two thousand lusty throats were giving vent to a deafening chorus of unbroken sound. The performer, expecting her customary warm ovation, was completely taken aback. She struggled to announce her first song, but it was a lost cause. The curtain was dropped and a little clutch of senior officers disappeared backstage to offer apologies. She refused to be placated, however, and within minutes her car was whisking her away in a huff to wherever she had come from. The rest of the show went ahead and, at the final curtain, the performers were treated to a show of enthusiasm far greater than their talent merited.

It was on the night of my first Passive Defence duty that I was to be given the cough treatment, though not, thankfully, on such a grand scale. We were all nicely settled in our seats and enjoying the first few minutes of the show when, over the tannoy system, came the piercing call: "Passive Defence Officer to muster watches. Passive Defence Officer to muster watches." I stood up to make my way out of the theatre and, immediately, the house lights came on and the show was stopped. Then, as I made for the door, the coughing started. I bowed my head to cover my embarrassment and stumbled out into the darkness in a state of confusion.

The next problem was finding the men who I was supposed to be commanding, for they were in three groups in various parts of the dockyard and I was by no means familiar with the layout of the area. Eventually, however, I spotted a small group of ratings who, at my approach, were brought to attention by a leading hand.

"Red Watch reporting, sir", he said. "All present and correct".

"Good", I replied. "Now, I suppose you all know your duties." "Yes, sir", said the leading hand.

I was rather relieved about that, for I certainly didn't.

Eventually, after about twenty minutes, I had succeeded in locating all three watches and, as there was no sign of any impending full alert, I decided I might as well return to the theatre and see the remainder of the show. It was as I quietly pushed open the little door that I received my next surprise, for all the lights were on and there was a steady buzz of conversation throughout the audience. I asssumed that it was the interval, but I couldn't have been more wrong. As I stepped inside, two thousand pairs of eyes turned in my direction. Then, almost immediately, two thousand pairs of hands met in a sudden burst of applause and two thousand lusty throats gave out with a spontaneous cheer.

What I was soon to realise was that they had, in fact, held up the show to await my return. Never since that night have I ever received such an overwhelming ovation.

CHAPTER 13
HMS Raleigh

One of the first people I had encountered when I arrived at HMS *Drake* was David Simpson, my old colleague from the London Hospital, who had reported a few weeks earlier. His experience proved very useful, for he was able to provide me with various hints and tips concerning our new lifestyle. There were many pitfalls to be avoided and nowhere was this more apparent than in the wardroom itself. This vast room, rather like the lounge of a gentlemen's club, was a popular socialising centre at lunchtime and again in the evening for a pre-prandial drink or two. It was there that I was to learn two important lessons.

The first was that there was a kind of apartheid system in operation, under which officers of different ranks were required to occupy certain pre-ordained areas. The part nearest the bar was the territory of commanders, captains and the occasional commodore or admiral. Next came the lieutenant commanders and then, occupying the largest section, the lieutenants. Sub-lieutenants, warrant officers and midshipmen tailed off towards the other end and, although there was no declared demarcation line, we were all expected to know our place. The only time we were permitted to stray into a higher station was by invitation from one of our superiors. This may sound rather like a sad reflection on a class-conscious society, but it was the way the Navy had always done it. It has to be admitted, indeed, that the system worked rather well, for we were all infinitely more relaxed amongst people of our own kind.

The second lesson which I lost no time in learning was that the wardroom could have a disastrous effect on one's personal cost of living. Our gross pay was 19/10d per day (less Income Tax, of course), out of which we were required to pay for our uniforms and other clothing and, almost unbelievably, our board and lodging. It was generally acknowledged that a senior rating was much better off than any officer under the rank of lieutenant commander, for he had these things provided for him by the Service.

Our great danger in the wardroom lay in the cost of purchases from the bar. It is generally believed that the Navy's traditional drink is rum but, while it is true that the ratings received their mid-morning tot, it was gin which found greatest favour amongst the officers. Stewards continually hovered in all corners of the room waiting for the slightest suggestion of a signal which would bring one of them gliding across with glasses of the coveted spirit. The great danger lay in the fact that, at that moment, no money actually changed hands. A chit would be produced, the purchaser would append his signature, and the innocent-looking slip of paper would be filed away to await the preparation of the monthly mess bill. It was then that disaster could strike for, unless one kept a tight rein on the number of chits one signed, it was highly probable that one's bank balance would not be capable of meeting the demands made upon it. I constantly marvelled at the manner in which some of my colleagues spent long hours imbibing that heady liquid without any apparent throught for the future.

My feeling of amazement became even greater on Guest Night, the weekly occasion on which relatives and friends could be invited on board for dinner. It was a peacetime tradition to which the officers of HMS *Drake* defiantly clung, carrying on their pretence that all was right with the world.

All the guests had to be officially approved and then, after drinks, the Commodore would lead the entire assembly, in strict order of seniority, into the Mess. Once there, the Padre would recite the Naval Grace, the strings and woodwinds of the Royal Marines' Band would strike up with "The Roast Beef of Old England" and the meal would proceed. We, of course, all wore our "tiddly suits". Gone was the serge and on had come the doeskin, together with wing collars and bow ties. Even the Wren stewards sported similar neckwear, together with white gloves which were so long that they reached almost to their armpits. All the while, up in the minstrels' gallery, the musicians played on and then came the Loyal Toast, for which we were allowed the singular privilege of remaining seated. It was a concession which had been granted centuries earlier when, in the confined quarters of the old wooden ships, Nelson's officers would have run the risk of knocking themselves unconscious by suddenly rising to their feet for the purpose. In the spaciousness of our Mess, it would have taken half a dozen of us standing on each other's shoulders to reach the ceiling, but still we carried on doing it the Navy way.

Though we all knew the origin of that tradition, I never discovered the reason why the port wine was never passed to the right. I only know that it was inclined to be inconvenient when the person on my immediate right wished to refill his glass and the decanter had to be sent on its long way round the table in the opposite direction.

There were times in that cocoon-like atmosphere when we had the greatest difficulty in remembering that, somewhere in the outside world, a war was going on. Whenever possible, however, we avoided Guest Night. We attended if we were on watch, for that was the only way we could get a meal. At other times we usually nipped ashore to Malcolm's, a local restaurant which was renowned for both the quality and quantity of its mixed grill.

It was during the course of one Guest Night, however, that I made the acquaintance of an R.A.F. Flight Lieutenant who had somehow found his way into the Mess and, as was usual on such occasions, we were soon busily engaged in extolling the virtues of our respective Services. While he was going into raptures about the thrill of flying through the air with no visible means of support, I was forced to confess that my fear of heights made it highly unlikely that I would ever wish to avail myself of that experience. Having said that, I regarded the matter as closed. He, however, had other ideas.

"If you're afraid of flying", he said, "there's only one way to cure it. Get up there and fly. Once you've been up there you'll never worry about it again."

I was far from convinced, but he was very persuasive and I found myself accepting his invitation to go up with him in a plane from his base. Thus it was that, a few days later, I set off on a borrowed bicycle for our rendezvous at Yelverton. I found the village with no undue trouble, but it was as I was pedalling along a country lane in search of the isolated airfield that I had a most unfortunate experience. It was a peaceful summer's evening with hardly a breath of wind and yet, suddenly and completely without warning, a hurricane of air tore violently across the lane, catching me completely in its path. It lifted both me and my machine bodily into the air, swept us sideways and deposited us on the opposite hedgebank. I was, naturally, somewhat taken aback, but the cause of the phenomenon was not long in making itself apparent. The roar of an aircraft engine soon told me that I had, in fact, reached my objective. It was simply a piece of sheer misfortune that I had chosen to cycle along just as somebody had brought one of the parked flying machines into life.

My host greeted me with a show of enthusiasm which I found great difficulty in sharing. He introduced me to the plane in which we were to set out on our adventure, and that was the moment when I really should have cut and run. I have no recollection of what type of aircraft it was, but it was very small and offered room for just the two of us. As we strapped ourselves in, I felt a distinct bond of sympathy with the humble sardine.

"Right", he said. "We're off", and, with that, we began trundling across the concrete runway. I found this part quite bearable; it was not until we actually parted company with the ground that the first real feeling of fear began to grip me. Then, as we went up in what seemed to be almost vertical flight, it reached proportions of near-panic and I grabbed hold of whatever support offered itself in that tiny cockpit. It was not until my host had reached the desired height and had put the aircraft into something approaching level flight that I realised I had left my stomach on the ground. It was several seconds before it finally came up and rejoined me.

I would dearly have loved to look down at the fields beneath us, but I was concentrating every nerve and sinew in an effort at survival. It was only when he banked the plane round in order to change course that I had my first involuntary glimpse of the Devonshire countryside.

I suppose our flight lasted for little more than ten minutes, but it seemed much longer. Then we were on the way down and I was convinced that we were approaching the ground much too quickly to be able to stop. I really should have had more faith in my pilot, for we touched down reasonably gently and, rolling along the airstrip, came to a halt. I was still holding on for dear life but, as he turned round towards me, his face beamed with gleeful pleasure.

"Well?" he said. "How was that?"

"Great", I said, lying through my teeth. "Just great!"

I staggered back with him to his mess quarters, where I sought relief with a cup of tea and a cigarette. It is difficult to exude an air of gaiety when one is in a state of near-collapse. Nevertheless, I couldn't possibly admit my true feelings. I had no desire to appear ungrateful and thus I tried, with forced application, to give the impression of great enthusiasm.

"There you are", he said. "I told you that once you got up there all your fears would disappear. Now, what you really want is another trip in a day or two, just to clinch it. What about it?"

"Great", I said. "That would be great. I'll give you a ring."

But, of course, I never did. Indeed, I made a point of avoiding the next few Guest Nights, just in case he might put in an appearance and try to inveigle me into repeating the torture. I had no wish to relive the torment of trying to defy the laws of gravity and, in any case, my time was fully occupied in coming to terms with the demands of my own Service.

At this point, lest it should be thought that the Navy was living in a world of fantasy far removed from the realities of war, I would hasten to add that it was only in a minority of aspects that such links with peacetime were maintained. Once we left the protective walls of the wardroom at HMS *Drake* all illusions were immediately shattered and this was to become particularly apparent when, in due course, we received our appointments to other farflung outposts.

Our new postings were not long delayed, for it was soon necessary for us to move on to other establishments in order to make room for the next intake. For two months we had been engaged in routine professional duties under the eagle eye of the Port Dental Officer, Surgeon Captain Lawry, a man with the reputation of being a stern disciplinarian. We found that reputation to be well-merited, although I had also discovered that this somewhat stern facade could readily be penetrated if one went the right way about it.

When I had put in my first request for weekend leave I had been warned that Captain Lawry regarded leave as a privilege rather than something to which we were automatically entitled. Thus, on the previous evening, I had carefully rehearsed the manner in which I would make my request; I put particular emphasis on my awareness of the fact that it was not a matter which could be taken for granted. My approach found such favour with him that not only did he immediately grant my request but he also offered the same privilege to my colleagues. From then on, he tended to regard me as the leader of our little group, a fact which was to stand me in good stead on future occasions.

When the signals began arriving with our new appointments, Captain Lawry handed them out rather in the manner of the Sovereign distributing maundy money. Each of my colleagues received two pieces of paper, one announcing the destination and the other being the travel warrant which would enable them to get there. When my appointment came through, however, there was no travel warrant.

"Just a short trip for you", said the Captain. "I'm keeping you near and handy."

It was, indeed, a short trip. It is true that it took me into a different county, but it involved merely crossing the river and going a few hundred yards down the road to Torpoint. There, on the west bank of the Tamar, was HMS *Raleigh*.

Life at *Raleigh* was a totally different concept from what had gone before. It was a New Entry Establishment into which, every six weeks or so, came a batch of seventeen-year-old lads to experience their first taste of Service life. Our job was to ease them through this initiation and to prepare them for what lay ahead. Thus we all had our appointed tasks, and we in the dental department were as busy as anybody.

The youngsters who formed our raw material came in a great diversity of types and from a wide variety of backgrounds. There were some whose dental condition had obviously been a matter of pride to their parents, and they gave us little trouble. There were many more, however, to whom a dental surgery was completely unexplored territory and, even worse, whose mouths had previously been no-go areas to such things as tooth brushes. With these, we spent long hours in an effort to rectify the years of neglect.

There was a widely-held belief among the new entrants that dental treatment was compulsory. We did little to dispel that myth although they were, in fact, allowed to refuse treatment if they so wished. Occasionally one of the lads would attempt to exercise that right, and it was then that time had to be spent advising him of the foolishness of his decision. Our master card was the fact that any such refusal was recorded on his Station Card. Then, if at any time he was unable to carry out his appointed duties because of an illness which might be linked with his dental condition, he could find himself in severe trouble. It was then classified as "self-inflicted injury", a serious offence in any of the Services.

The young lads were treated with great consideration during their early weeks and, indeed, were even allowed to pack up and go home if they decided that the Navy was too much for them. This action, however, gained them little for, having reached call-up age, they would then have been automatically drafted into the Army. Much counselling was done whenever signs of homesickness came to the surface, and it was then that our padres came into their own.

110

We were well served with "sky pilots", and there was one in particular with whom I developed a close link. He was very new to the Service and, indeed, to the ministry, and he was full of the enthusiasm of the freshly-ordained curate. The only trouble was that his bubbling nature sometimes got the better of him and he had a marked tendency towards speaking without first considering the implications of what he said. As a result, he often found himself in an embarrassing situation of his own making.

One such incident occurred during one of our Open Days, when relatives of our young charges were encouraged to come aboard and find out how their offspring were being treated. The padre and I were strolling among the guests when he suddenly spotted a woman with a young baby in her arms. One glimpse was all he needed and he was diving in feet first.

"What a bonny baby", he said. "You must be proud to have such a beautiful grandchild."

"Grandchild be blowed", replied the woman. "I'm its mother!"

It was just one of a multitude of bricks which he dropped as he made his effervescent way through his Naval ministry. I often wondered how he would fare when he moved on to other surroundings, but I need have had no misgivings on that score. Within nine months he was decorated for gallantry on the beaches of Normandy.

CHAPTER 14
Aaron and Rebecca

Our base at *Raleigh* covered a vast area and spread far and wide into the surrounding countryside. Thus it was that my boyhood love of walking stood me in good stead, for we had little in the way of wheeled transport to assist us in our daily journeyings. There were one or two trucks, together with the odd jeep, but these were reserved for the carriage of goods rather than human cargoes.

There was, however, a certain form of transport which became available to me and one which was destined to play a significant part in my explorations of the countryside which surrounded us. This was the "station bike". It was the most basic of all bicycles, built solely for strength and with no concessions to comfort or speed. It was of solid construction and heavy in the extreme but, apart from wheels, it had none of the attributes of the normal cycle. The saddle was devoid of springs and, because the machine was designed solely for use on the base, it did not possess any kind of lighting system. Worst of all, however, was the fact that it had no brakes. The only way to bring the machine to a halt was to put one's feet on the floor and dig in one's heels. This worked quite well on a reasonably soft surface but, on concrete roads, it tended to play havoc with one's footwear.

There were, in fact, three of these machines, all painted in a vivid shade of pillarbox red in order to deter the criminal fraternity from thoughts of theft. This, however, failed to prevent me from appropriating one of them and putting it to my own use.

Riding the vehicle was, in the early stages, something of a penance. At the time I likened it to a battle of wits with an unbroken colt although later experience led more to a comparison with a pig-headed Suffolk Punch. Eventually, however, the lower part of my body accustomed itself to the continual physical battering which every encounter brought with it, and I used the monstrous machine to take me out into the Cornish countryside. To allay suspicion, I always set off down the road in the direction of another Naval establishment which was situated not more than a mile away. Then I would peel off into whichever direction my fancy demanded as

112

I set myself the task of discovering whether the beauty of those little Cornish villages matched that of their names. Thus it was that I made the acquaintance of such as St. Germans and Polbathick, Downderry and Portwrinkle and, probably my favourites, Kingsand and Cawsand.

It was during one of the many excursions which I made on my old station bike that I made the acquaintance of two of the loveliest people it has ever been my good fortune to meet. It was one of those days in late August when the sun shone and the sky was as blue as a dunnock's egg. I had an afternoon free of duty and I set off down the road from *Raleigh* determined to make the most of my brief spell of freedom. I knew exactly where I was going, for I had been there many times before. Inland I rode below the quiet St. Germans River and then, turning left, on through the country lanes to the twin villages of Kingsand and Cawsand. There, at a vantage point which I had discovered on previous visits, I laid aside my bicycle and sat back to gaze over the deceptively quiet waters of Cawsand Bay.

I call them deceptively quiet for, although they presented an outer aspect of utter tranquillity, it was well known that the underwater currents carried hidden dangers for the unsuspecting swimmer. Quite a number of lives had been lost in those treacherous waters, and the practice of swimming in Cawsand Bay was, indeed, prohibited as far as Naval personnel were concerned. This ban, however, was not always respected and, as I looked down from my elevated viewpoint, I could see a little group of sailors and Wrens disporting themselves in those tempting waters. I paid them little heed, however, as I lay back in blissful contemplation of the vista out past Penlee Point and further on to the open waters of the English Channel. This, for me, was the happier side of war and I reflected upon my good fortune. I knew only too well that so many others, under that very same sun, were finding life far from comfortable.

I cannot recall how long I lay there but eventually, as the sun headed for its nocturnal resting place, I decided to take similar action. I lifted up my bicycle and set forth on my return journey.

It was as I approached the little village of St. John that I became aware of an increasing feeling of thirst, and I accordingly made up my mind to rectify the matter. On previous trips I had seen the tiny inn which served the needs of the local menfolk, but I had never before entered within its walls. As I opened the door and stepped inside I cannot, in all honesty, say that my arrival was greeted with any outward show of enthusiasm by the occupants. Later visits were destined to give me many hours of extreme pleasure, but there was no hint of that on this occasion. Six heads turned in unison towards the door and six pairs of eyes gave me the most cursory of glances. Then, just as quickly, they reverted to whatever had held their attention before my invasion of their privacy.

I settled for half a pint of the local cider. I knew full well that anything less than a pint was regarded hereabouts as a child's drink, but I had had earlier experience of that powerful liquid and had good reason to respect its potency. I took the mug in my hand and turned to survey the scene. The men were huddled in intimate discussion and I was immediately struck by the solidity of their physique, an attribute which was reflected by the furniture at which they sat. They were craggy and weather-beaten, and each gave a distinct impression of having been hewn from solid granite. Only one looked any different from the rest and it was he, sitting on the end of a wooden settle at the far side of the room, who first acknowledged my presence. He was an old man, as weather-worn as the others, with bleach-white hair and a ruddy face which gave me a smile of welcome.

"Come over here and sit by me, lad", he said.

I accepted his invitation, not knowing that it was destined to be the first move towards a bond of intimate friendship. This was Aaron, with whom I was to share a multitude of happy hours over the ensuing months.

Aaron had lived all his eighty-odd years within shouting distance of the sea, yet he had never ventured out onto those treacherous waters. He was a landsman and had spent all his life tilling, sowing and harvesting the richness of the soil. His companions had all been fishermen, sailing out to reap the harvest of the sea, and, when they heard the reason for my presence in their midst, they accepted me with warmth and enthusiasm. It mattered little to them that I was just a land-locked dentist. I was "in the Navy" and, in their eyes, that made me only one thing – a sailor. Thus was I welcomed by my newly-found friends.

The strongest bond, however, was to be between me and Aaron, and it started its development that very evening as we left the inn together. He told me that it was his practice, once a week, to take home some fish and chips for supper and he invited me to share that meal with him and his wife. Needless to say, I accepted his invitation without hesitation and so, in due course, we trudged along the little lane which led to his cottage. There, for the first time, I was to meet Rebecca. At least, I assumed that was her name but, in truth, I never heard Aaron use the first syllable. He was as economical in speech as he was in most other things and, when he spoke of her, it was always just as "Becca".

Becca, for her part, never used Aaron's name at all when speaking of him. To her he was simply "my man", and this aptly described their relationship. They had gone through life together for more than sixty years and they had reached the stage of being rather like two bodies with a single spirit. When Aaron strolled down to the inn each evening Becca knew that he would be happy in the company of his friends, and thus she was happy. She would sit in peaceful contemplation, darning or sewing, until she heard the sound of footsteps which told her that her man was back. During the day while Aaron cultivated his vegetable garden and tended the flock of chickens and the single cow which he kept out at the back, Becca would do her cleaning and baking. Once a week she would carry out her "churning", producing the richest, creamiest butter I have ever tasted. All the while, her placid temperament took her along in an atmosphere of unruffled calm.

The only time I ever saw the slightest suggestion of a hiccup in her steady passage through life was when I stood inside her little parlour on that very first visit. She immediately went into a burst of bustling activity, gently chiding poor Aaron as she did so.

"If I'd known you were bringing company home", she said, "I would have got the best tablecloth out."

That tablecloth was one of her most highly prized possessions. Painstakingly worked in hand-stitched lace, it had been given to her by her mother for her "bottom drawer" way back in 1882. It had obviously been used only on very rare occasions, for it still retained the appearance of freshness which it had possessed when it was first folded in tissue paper and lovingly stored away. I was destined to see quite a lot of that tablecloth during the months which followed, for it was always on the table when I shared a meal with Aaron and Becca. This unfortunately meant that I always had a slight feeling of unease, for I felt sure that, at some stage in the proceedings, I would do something stupid like knocking over a cup of tea or dropping a buttered scone the wrong side up.

Over the next few months my association with that delightful couple was to be a source of great joy to me. It was also destined to give me a deep insight into the effect which mutual love can have upon the lives of two people who share it, for Aaron and Becca were more deeply in love than any other couple I have ever known, either before or since. In truth, that love was just about all they possessed, for their material possessions were meagre and, saddest of all, they had no living relatives. It is true that everybody in the village was a friend, but they had had no closer relationship since their only son had gone away as cannon fodder in the Great War. I had learned of his existence after commenting upon the solitary photograph which stood upon the mantelpiece. It was typical of the many which had been taken just twenty-five years earlier, with the young man in his stiff new uniform trying to force a weak smile to provide loved ones with a fond memory as he went off to fight the Kaiser. I failed to learn his name, for they never referred to him again. I only know that, like so many of his generation, he had sailed away to France in 1914 and, within two short weeks, had become just another statistic in the ever-mounting casualty lists. Since then, they had lived their lives in a spirit of simple, undemanding partnership, regularly thanking their Maker for his goodness, and that little cottage was destined to draw me back many times in the months which followed.

It was during those later visits that I was to be given an insight into another, though somewhat contrasting, facet of local life – the art of playing dominoes. In my Norfolk boyhood I had received the game as a Christmas present and had derived childish pleasure from engaging my brothers in simple challenge matches. We had known little of the rules and were happy simply to try and match the spots. Here in the Cornish countryside, however, it was a totally different concept. It was, in fact, the major local sport. Each village had its own team, together with the most ardent band of supporters one could ever have encountered. To them, the result of the previous night's match was a far more significant talking point than the chances of England beating Australia at cricket or of Tottenham Hotspur winning the F.A. Cup. Local honour was at stake and, consequently, dominoes was a very serious matter.

The cause of my introduction to the domino fraternity was the fact that Aaron was a member of the local team. Indeed, I do him less than justice by describing him simply as a member, for he was accepted as their star player. Furthermore, when he took part in a match he was a totally different man from the one we otherwise knew. As he sat at that pub bench, a cluster of the little black pieces

116

clutched in his fist, all trace of emotion would disappear from his face. Gone was the beaming countenance with the ever-ready smile, to be replaced by the sternest, most expressionless features imagineable. He would surely have made a first-class poker player! For the entire duration of the match not a single facial muscle would move as he dedicated his entire being to the task of trying to outwit his opponent. Then, when it was all over, he was back to his old self as, with his team mates, he would discuss various aspects of the match and speculate as to what would have happened if a certain player had done this, or that, or the other.

His enthusiasm for the game stirred my interest and he began to teach me its finer points. I think I must have been a fairly receptive pupil for, some time later, I was offered a place in the team. I had certain qualms about accepting, for my own belief in my ability did not quite match theirs. I could not possibly decline, however, for this was the greatest honour which they could confer on any man, and the fact that I, as a "foreigner", was being recognised in such a way added greatly to its significance.

I am not quite sure whether I derived as much satisfaction from the matches as did my colleagues, for I experienced a certain difficulty in approaching the encounters with their high degree of reverence. In spite of this, however, I believe I managed to justify my team mates' confidence in my ability. Certainly, my presence in the team was to bring me many hours of pleasureable enjoyment, a fact which caused a certain degree of wonderment amongst my colleagues at *Raleigh*.

One of them, a Surgeon Lieutenant by the name of Peter Lawson, continually pumped me concerning my frequent incursions into the local countryside and expressed the wish that he might accompany me. He was a nice enough chap but, to be perfectly honest, I had a distinct preference for my own company on such occasions. However, the fact that Lawson and I were on the same watch meant that our off-duty periods usually coincided, so I grudgingly yielded to his request. I did, however, set him two conditions. To begin with, it would be necessary for him to appropriate one of the remaining station bikes and then, having done so, he must be prepared to endure the physical torture which his use of the machine would bring with it. He fulfilled both of these demands and thus it was that, one afternoon, two figures could have been seen pedalling their strange machines along the country lanes of Cornwall.

I should, perhaps, explain that Lawson was a small man with a somewhat ruddy complexion and a penchant for living his life at a modest pace. At no time did he ever show any outward sign of excitement or emotion and he appeared to have the firm conviction that energy should be used as economically as possible. Thus it was that the early stages of our ride were conducted at speeds which varied between slow, dead slow and complete inertia. The only change in his outward appearance was that the ruddiness of his complexion quickly became even more pronounced, giving the distinct impression that his face had been sprayed with the same bright red paint which adorned the frame of his bicycle. Nevertheless, we gradually settled down to a modest rate of progress and I eventually succeeded in getting him as far as Cawsand. The look of pleasure on Lawson's face as he flung aside his bicycle and collapsed on the grass was something which defied description.

"Riding that bike", he said, "is like banging your head against a brick wall – it's lovely when you leave off!"

I was about to remind him that we still had to face the return journey when suddenly, and completely without warning, he collapsed on his back and fell fast asleep.

By the time we began our homeward run, the last rays of daylight were beginning to fade and the moon had begun its journey across the sky. We were glad of the moon's presence, for it was the only illumination we had as we made our way through Cawsand and on to St. John. By now, Lawson had settled into some kind of faltering rhythm, but then, with startling suddenness, our steady progress was shattered by the strident call of a man's voice.

"Ahoy there!"

We dug our heels into the ground in unison and brought our machines to a halt. Our two heads turned as one in the direction from which the sound had come. There was no mistaking the familiar form of the village constable standing there in the moonlit distance.

It was then that I was confronted by a sight which I would never have believed possible if I had not personally witnessed it. Lawson put his bike into motion and, with all the speed and directness of a missile ejected from a catapult, sped off into the distance. Indeed, the proverbial scalded cat would have had difficulty in keeping up with him as he pedalled furiously up the hill and disappeared into the darkness. It was a show of sheer physical energy, the like of which I would never have believed could have been within his capability, and it was not until the next morning that I learned what had prompted such a magnificent performance.

It seems that, on seeing the sudden appearance of the constable, he had assumed that we were about to be brought to book for such dastardly crimes as riding without lights and having no brakes. What he did not realise was that the worthy officer was, in fact, a member of the dominoes team and he merely wished to ensure that I was aware of arrangements for the next match. For a variety of reasons, all of which must by now be readily apparent, Lawson never again expressed the wish to accompany me on one of my jaunts.

My happy association with the good folk of St. John came to an end when I left *Raleigh* for another appointment. I took my leave of them with the promise that I would return as soon as circumstances allowed. As luck would have it, I was able to keep that promise sooner than I had expected for, within a few months, I was back at Devonport.

I crossed the river on the Torpoint ferry and, on the other side, I scrounged a lift in a jeep with one of the American soldiers who had, by then, taken over that part of Cornwall. I had not expected to find any changes in the village in such a short time and, at least from the outside, it was just the same as when I had last seen it. When I came to that little cottage, however, I found the cruellest change of all, for it stood empty. The two dear people who had spent so many years within its walls were there no more.

It transpired that Becca had taken to her bed with pneumonia a few weeks earlier and, lacking the strength to overcome it, had gone peacefully to sleep. And what of Aaron? Within forty-eight hours he had followed her.

Nobody knew for certain the cause of Aaron's death. Could it be that "Broken Heart" would not be considered a sufficiently professional diagnosis for a doctor's certificate?

CHAPTER 15

Cornish Pasties and Commandos

The passage of time in the Navy is denoted, not by means of a clock, but by striking the ship's bell every half-hour. The rule is that the bell receives one stroke at 4.30, 8.30 and 12.30, with one more stroke being added for each half-hour until eight strokes are reached at 8, 12 and 4 o'clock. Then the process starts again. The ringing of the bell was a routine part of our lives, just as the striking of the church clock is to a country community. There was one occasion, however, when for me it was destined to take on a somewhat greater significance.

The sound of eight bells ringing out at midnight was normally of interest only to those who, having completed their duty on the first watch, were then due to be relieved by the middle watch. On New Year's Eve, however, things were slightly different, for it was then the custom to give eight bells for the old year and another eight for the new one. Thus, on that one night, sixteen bells would ring out across the ship. Furthermore, it was the tradition that the ringing of the bell on that occasion should be carried out, not by the quartermaster, but by the youngest officer in the wardroom. Nothing had been said to me, but I knew myself to be the youngest officer. Thus, when New Year's Eve duly arrived, I viewed the prospect with a certain degree of foreboding.

My main worry concerned my ability to carry out the task, for it was not a simple one. When one started striking the clapper against the inside of the bell it started to sway, and this motion increased with every additional strike until, by eight bells, the whole thing was swaying violently. To reach sixteen seemed a physical impossibility, and there was no way in which I could even manage a practice session.

I decided that the first essential was to stay completely sober. Thus, as the evening wore on, I sat in the mess casually reading the newspapers and watching my colleagues as they progressed through varying stages of intoxication. Time went steadily past and, when nothing had been said by 11.30, I started telling myself that my fears had been groundless. I began to feel relaxed, but it was then that my hopes were shattered.

"Alright, Toothy", said the First Lieutenant. "I think it's time we started getting you ready."

With that, he proceeded to strap a pair of gaiters round my ankles and, much worse, a sword around my waist. It was by no means a simple operation, for he was completely and utterly inebriated. When he had satisfied himself with my appearance, he led me outside to where an escort of ratings was waiting to take me to the place of execution. To say that we marched there would be an exaggeration in the case of the First Lieutenant. However, we eventually reached our destination and there was the quartermaster awaiting our arrival.

We took up our places around the bell and, as I awaited the fateful moment, I held the clapper firmly at the ready. Then, at the given signal, I launched into my performance. I gave the bell two gentle strikes, then two more and then a further two. It was swinging wider and wider and I was having difficulty in making contact. I struggled past eight bells and it was then that the First Lieutenant decided that I was in need of help. He grabbed my hand and swung drunkenly at the bell, which gave out a medley of sound such as had never before been heard from such an instrument. Then, dragging me with him, he collapsed on the ground in a heap. A chorus of tittering went through the ranks of our escort, but the First Lieutenant just looked at me and smiled.

"Well", he said. "I think there should have been sixteen somewhere amongst that lot."

I could do nothing more than hope that I would never again be the youngest officer in the wardroom on New Year's Eve.

As the early months of 1944 slipped by, there was a growing demand for the opening of a Second Front, and it seemed only a matter of time before some sort of landing would be attempted on the coast of Europe. The build-up of forces went on at an ever-increasing rate and we found ourselves having to deal with large numbers of personnel from other bases as well as our own intake. This extra volume of work frequently involved carrying on well into the night and it was inevitable that it should eventually begin to take its toll. One by one we began to give way under the strain. In my own case it was rather frightening, for I awoke one morning to find out that I had, to all intents and purposes, gone blind overnight. I was not completely sightless, for I could make out shapes and colours, but I was unable to bring any of them into focus. I found myself lost in a kind of dream world.

The result was a spell in Stonehouse Naval Hospital at Plymouth where, after a few weeks, my sight was restored more or less to normal. Whilst there, I made the acquaintance of a young midshipman who had just parted company with his appendix, and eventually he and I travelled up to London together on sick leave. We were alone in the compartment until shortly before the train was due to leave, but then we were joined by a lady of mature years who took her place on the opposite seat.

We always found that civilians in the West Country were very good at offering hospitality to servicemen, and this lady was no exception. To be perfectly honest, we would have been much happier on our own, for we were quite content with each other's company. It was not to be, however, for our new companion wasted no time in engaging us in conversation. She was particularly keen to know our opinion of Plymouth and it was soon apparent that she had a deep love of the place.

"Of course", she said, "you won't have known it before the bombing", and, with that, she produced a huge pile of photographs of Plymouth as it was before the Luftwaffe had ravaged it in 1941. We waded through them all and tried to make appropriate comments, but it was not the Plymouth we knew, with its shattered streets and bomb sites.

"But", she assured us, "Plymouth will rise again and be even more beautiful than it was before."

We marvelled at her confidence, for we were not to know that she was somebody with a great influence on the future of the city. By the time we had finished our review of pre-war Plymouth we were well on our journey, and it was then that she made her next move.

"Now, what have you boys got to eat?" she asked.

We told her that we had nothing, but we assured her that we would have a meal when we reached London.

"Not a bit of it", she said. "You must share my pasties. I made them myself last night – they're the real thing, made to the traditional Cornish recipe."

Now, there are many things that I love about Cornwall, but the pasty is not one of them. There is something about it which does not appeal to my sense of taste, but the dear lady would not be thwarted. She produced her home-made confections and I must confess that they went down rather well.

Before long we were drawing near our destination and it was only then that we became aware of the identity of our hostess. As she put the photographs back in one of her bags we spotted the little label announcing the name of its owner. It was Lady Astor.

We bade our farewells to our benefactor and then, at the end of the platform, the middy and I parted company. What we did not know was that, a few months later and under very different conditions, our paths were once again destined to cross.

One of the most significant features of the great build-up of troops in the area at that time was the presence among them of large numbers of Americans. To some of the civilian population they were symbols of glamour from across the sea, but the Navy did not regard them quite in the same light. Thus, while the children of Plymouth were soon to be seen perpetually chewing vast quantities of gum and many local young ladies sported newly-acquired nylon stockings, the average sailor welcomed the arrival of the Yanks with something less than enthusiasm. For one thing, they were very highly-paid and even the humblest G.I. had a degree of affluence to which the average British serviceman could never aspire. Then there was the manner of their lifestyle, and it was this which was to cause me personal discomfort when, on arriving back from sick leave, I found that half a dozen American Army officers had taken up residence in our Mess.

There was one in particular, a certain Captain Frasier, who immediately announced that he wanted to be my friend. Now, I am quite happy for anybody to be my friend, but I find it slightly disconcerting when somebody declares it to be his avowed intention at the outset of one's very first meeting. Furthermore, I had already suffered a similar unsolicited friendship with a mad Australian lieutenant named Norman Phillips. The reason for his presence in our midst had never become apparent to us, but we were all well aware that he was completely "round the bend". The fact that he, also, was aware of his mental condition is borne out by the further fact that he invented for himself the nickname of "Dnieper", a reference to the Battle of the Dnieper Bend which was raging in Russia at that time. His outrageous behaviour, even in public places, made him the sort of person whom one would not willingly introduce to one's maiden aunt, and relief only came

Norman E. Phillips. R.A.N.

To Baggie from Dnisher. 19·3·44.

HMS "Raleigh".

Round the Bend.

Lieutenant Phillips, R.A.N.

Captain Frasier, U.S. Army

Shipmates at Raleigh. My two unwelcome friends are in the middle, and on the right is the young padre who tended to create embarrassing situations for himself.

when he eventually moved on to some other unsuspecting ward-room.

My joy was short-lived, however, for, with the arrival of the U.S. Army, I now found myself in a similar situation with the diminutive Captain Frasier. It was a very one-sided arrangement from the outset and the fact that he insisted on accompanying me wherever I went in my off-duty time was a source of great annoyance. Then there were his eating habits which, though accepted as normal by his compatriots, were somewhat disconcerting to the rest of us. It is true that, for breakfast, he would partake of sausages, kippers or whatever fare we normally had. What caused us personal discomfort, however, was the fact that, before eating them, he would spread them with jam or marmalade, a combination which, to us, was nauseating in the extreme. Then there was his habit of smoking a cigarette between the various courses of a meal, a practice hitherto unheard of in our Mess.

Over the ensuing weeks conditions became steadily worse as more Americans arrived and we learned that they were, in fact, preparing to take over HMS *Raleigh* as a U.S. military establishment. Before long we were outnumbered by the newcomers and every aspect of our lives, including catering, was changed to the American way of doing things. It was at this point that I decided that I had had enough and I put in a request to Captain Lawry for a new appointment. To my great relief, it arrived within a matter of days. It was only when I learned the nature of my new post that I had certain misgivings, for I was to be Dental Officer to a Royal Marines commando unit at Lympstone in Devon. After due consideration, however, I decided that even this would be preferable to submitting to the strange lifestyle of our allies from across the ocean.

The Royal Marines are something of a hybrid species for, though technically neither sailors nor soldiers, they are, in effect, a combination of both. When they shared a Naval mess they conformed largely to our routine and they were often subjected to much light-hearted banter as to their lack of identity. They retaliated by claiming that they had the best of both worlds in that they were employed by the Navy but paid by the Army.

In their own setting, as I soon discovered when I arrived at Lympstone, they conducted themselves in a very military manner and, what is more, they expected me to conform. There were two other toothies, and the three of us waged a continual battle in an effort to cling to our Naval roots. There were, however, many aspects in which we had to concede defeat.

The most frightening revelation concerning my new situation came shortly after my arrival with the realisation that I was not there just to provide routine dental treatment. All three of us had been picked because of our experience with jaw fractures and similar injuries and, though strictly non-combatant officers, we were now inextricably linked to our own individual commando unit. Thus, wherever my group went, I would have to accompany them. The trouble was that they were, at that moment, training for imminent landings on the coast of Europe. The idea of being suddenly dumped on some heavily fortified enemy stronghold did not fill me with enthusiasm. I had told Captain Lawry that I would like to be a bit closer to the action, but I hadn't meant that close. I found my new situation somewhat lacking in appeal.

My enthusiasm waned even more when I learned that, as part of my initiation, I would be required to negotiate the assault course. This gruesome collection of obstacles, running almost completely round the perimeter of the camp, had obviously been designed by somebody with a highly-inflated estimation of the physical capabilities of a normal human being. It was, in fact, that very assault course which had been the cause of my arrival at Lympstone, for I was taking the place of a toothy who had broken his arm in trying to meet its demands. There was no escape, however, and I approached the challenge with a mixture of foreboding and resignation.

I was led to the starting point by a Marine instructor who professed a confidence in my ability which I found great difficulty in sharing. He was a disgustingly fit young man who could obviously have ambled round the course in his sleep. My fears, however, increased as I neared the obstacles and realised that they were much larger in close-up than they had appeared from a distance.

"Ready Sir?" he asked.

"As ready as I ever will be", I replied.

"Right", he said and, with a shrill blast of his whistle, he set me on my way.

The first obstacle was a grass-covered mound which was not too demanding if one took it steadily. Then, however, as I stood on the top and looked forward to the next hazard, I nearly gave in on the spot. It was the brick wall, and I had not realised how tall it was.

The idea crossed my mind that I ought to have worn gloves, but there was no time to dwell on the matter. I ran down the slope, took a gigantic leap upwards and managed to get my hands on the top of the wall. Then came the difficult part of trying to manoeuvre the rest of my body on to the wall and, by the time I had done that, I was completely exhausted. I straddled the top of the obstacle, trying to regain my breath before dropping down the other side, and it was then that I heard the instructor's voice calling up to me.

"Don't worry", he said. "It's only pain!"

I dropped down, and then it was a question of crawling along the ground under a stretch of netting. By the time I had accomplished that, the instructor was out of my sight, and I proceeded on my way at a leisurely pace. Eventually there came relief in the form of the last obstacle, and there was my tormentor, whistle in one hand and stopwatch in the other, waiting to receive me. What I had not realised was that he had been watching my progress through binoculars.

"How did I do?" I asked.

"You made very good time, Sir", he said. "The only trouble is that you went under everything you should have gone over, and over everything you should have gone under."

I knew only too well that, if I had been a Marine, I would have had to repeat the ordeal many times until I satisfied him. We left it at that, however, for we both knew he had been on a loser right from the start.

The military nature of the establishment affected every facet of our lives and even made its presence felt in our living quarters where, instead of an officer's steward, I now had a batman. I had never before come across this species of person and it was a total revelation. The man appointed to my service was truly a "gentleman's gentleman", with a dedication to his work which transformed it from mere duty into a lifetime's vocation. He went about his duties with an air of authority and a degree of meticulous precision which suggested that he was supervising affairs in some stately home rather than in my modest little cabin. Furthermore, he had very firm views concerning the manner in which an officer should conduct himself, particularly in matters of dress.

Every morning, precisely at seven o'clock, he would enter my cabin and place a cup of tea beside my bed. Then, as he left, he would take my uniform from its hanger and retire to his quarters, where he would press the lapels of my jacket and deal similarly with the creases in my trousers. Even worse, he would reject the shirt I had worn the previous day and lay out a clean one ready for my use. I must confess that I had not been in the habit of wearing a clean shirt every day and I soon found that this practice played havoc with my laundry bill. I therefore suggested to him that we were taking things to extremes and perhaps I might make a shirt last two days, but I immediately regretted my action. His face, normally so expressionless, took on a look of pained surprise which made it plain that I had offended his innermost feelings.

"I like to see my officers properly turned out at all times", he said, with a hint of reproach in his voice.

I experienced a strong feeling of guilt and, henceforth, I found myself forever trying to please him. There could be no doubt that he had taken over my life and I had no option other than to face up to the increased cost of meeting his standards. All the while, however, he attended to my needs with an ever-present urge to give satisfaction. One day, in the Mess, he approached me with the request for "A word in your ear, Sir". I inclined my head to hear what it was that he wanted to say.

"I believe Sir is going on leave tomorrow", he said.

"Yes", I replied. "Just for the weekend."

"I take it that Sir will be requiring the usual?" he said.

I had no idea what "the usual" was, but I had no wish to show my ignorance, so I answered in the affirmative. The next morning all was revealed, for there in my cabin was a cardboard box containing a dressed chicken, a joint of meat and a bottle each of whisky and gin. I have no idea of his source of supply, but it was certainly not Black Market, for the charge was modest. It was just part of his continual desire to look after his officers.

Meanwhile, the Marines continued their training and I maintained the fervent hope that my injured colleague would return before anything drastic happened. Eventually my hopes were realised and it was time for me to take my leave of Lympstone. I wondered where my next appointment would take me and, when the signal came through, I had difficulty in believing my luck, for I was to get my first ship.

I was amazed at my good fortune for, when I had first arrived at Devonport, I had been told in no uncertain terms that no toothy ever got a sea-going appointment for at least two years. Only the larger ships carried dental officers and there was always great competition for such a post. To add to my feeling of excitement there was the fact that it was not just any old ship which I was joining. It was, in fact, HMS *King George V*, a battleship which was the pride of the Fleet. She was a truly massive creature, with a displacement of 35,000 tons and a complement of 1,500 officers and men. I rejoiced at the thought that I was about to become one of that company.

HMS King George V

I made my way to the dock at Devonport where she lay and, even as I got my first distant view of her, I felt a surge of pleasure at the thought of spending the next year or two within her walls. As I made my way on board I had great difficulty in controlling my excitement, but it was then that Fate dealt me a cruel blow. There had been an administrative mix-up and two of us had received the same appointment. The other was a Surgeon Lieutenant Commander Bradshaw, an officer with far greater seniority than me, and it was he, of course, who took up the position. The fact that I was invited to spend the day aboard savouring big-ship routine for the first time did little to ease my disappointment. If anything, it made things worse, for I became steadily aware of what had been cruelly snatched from my grasp.

I then had no alternative other than to report back to Captain Lawry and throw myself upon his mercy. He was full of sympathy, but he had little else to offer other than the normal dockyard routine. There was only one little bit of light relief available and this was in the form of part-time duties at the Wrens' Sick Bay. I felt it to be something of a contrast to sailing the high seas on the *K.G.V.*, but at least it would add a little variety to my life. Grudgingly, and with a distinct lack of enthusiasm, I took up my new duties.

130

CHAPTER 16
The Hand Of Fate

The most formidable hazard one was likely to encounter during one's incursions into the Wrens' Sick Bay was the Sister-in-Charge. Her reputation was such that she was always spoken about in hushed tones, verging on the reverential, for Sister was as formidable as any of her civilian counterparts. Indeed, it could truly be said that she was even more so, for she exhibited a never-failing presence which indicated to all comers that the Sick Bay was her territory and hers alone.

Her nursing staff were no problem to her, for they were fairly permanent fixtures and this meant that she had had plenty of time to mould them into the kind of force which best suited her regime. Medical and dental officers, however, were a totally different concept for, because of the demands of the Service, they were frequently changing. Accordingly, she tolerated their intrusion into her domain with such good grace as she could muster, whilst always making it patently clear that she regarded their presence on her ward as something of a nuisance. It was not that she ever expressed her feelings verbally; her method was much more subtle. Just a slight wrinkling of the nose or the suggestion of an upward curl at one side of her mouth conveyed her exasperation more forcibly than a thousand words.

Thus we were always on our guard. Never did we feel relaxed until we had finished our rounds and were able to leave her territory for the comparative sanity of the wardroom. There we would seek the relaxing comfort of a stiff gin, bringing with it a soothing of the nerves and a reduction of the blood pressure which enabled us to face the next call of duty.

In fairness to Sister, it must be said that the tensions of Sick Bay routine did not all stem from the rigours of her dictatorship. Some, indeed, arose from the patients themselves. It is undoubtedly true that many of the young ladies who joined the W.R.N.S. did so with the highest of motives. Many, indeed, performed a valuable service to their country in a wide range of activities such as had previously been unknown in the history of the Royal Navy. Others, of course,

131

were inspired by a spirit of adventure and a desire to widen their horizons. Then, it must be added, there were those who regarded the Service as a promising hunting ground in which to look for a husband. They may well have represented a very small minority, but they nevertheless popped up all over the place. And one of the places where they surfaced was in the Wrens' Sick Bay.

Medical officers were, of course, frequent visitors, and what better catch could there be than a young doctor? Dental officers probably occupied a slightly lower position in their list of desirables, but even one of those would be most acceptable as a possible future husband. That being so, what better place could there be for setting out their stalls than a bed in Sick Bay?

My predecessor in office had warned me of the presence of members of this predatory species and had provided graphic details of the methods they employed in furtherance of their aims. I must confess I paid little heed to his admonitions concerning the need for constant vigilance, for he was the kind of character who was prone to exaggeration in most things. It took only the barest minimum of time, however, for me to be brought face to face with the wisdom of his advice. It happened, in fact, on my very first visit to Sick Bay.

There were two patients who needed my attention and Sister had everything under control. She took me in tow rather in the manner of a tractor pulling a disc harrow and piloted me to the first bed just inside the door. There sat this poor girl, with her lower jaw held in her hand and a look of utter misery on her face. She had lost a filling and was suffering agonies as a result. Replacing the filling at the bedside was not feasible, so I decided to insert a sedative dressing. I set myself to the task, with Sister breathing heavily down my neck and exhibiting her usual air of impatience. Then, with the dressing in place, it was merely a question of ensuring that the tooth remained reasonably dry until the hardening process was complete.

Then, as I held my patient's lower jaw in my hands, I raised my eyes for the first time and suddenly became aware that two dozen pairs of eyes had been watching my every move. The supreme confidence which I had earlier developed during my ward rounds at the London Hospital seemed to have evaporated somewhat, but I battled on. As I stood there, I let my eyes wander idly around the ward, looking at nothing in particular. Suddenly, however, my air of assumed nonchalance fell in tatters as I beheld a vision in the bed

132

at the far end of the ward. I can only describe her as the healthiest-looking patient I had ever seen sitting in a hospital bed. With face meticulously made up and hair neatly brushed, she stood out in stark contrast to all her wardmates. Above all, however, it was the nature of her attire which caused shock waves to assail my senses for, in contrast to the sturdy flannelette which clothed most of the other patients, she wore a nightie which would have been more in keeping with a honeymoon hotel than the Wrens' Sick Bay. Decorated with bows and frills, it was made of a material which I can only describe as diaphanous. It was, to say the least, slightly revealing, and it was then that I remembered my predecessor's warning. This was obviously one of "them".

My brain quickly went into overdrive to find a way of dealing with the situation, but such action was unnecessary, for Sister's eyes had been following mine and her voice rang out across the ward with all the raucousness of a klaxon horn.

"Nurse", she yelled. "Tell that girl to cover herself up!"

My eyes returned to my patient who, by now, was declaring that she was free of pain. Certainly she looked infinitely happier than when I first saw her.

Then it was on to the next patient and, as Sister escorted me down the central aisle between the beds, I kept my gaze firmly fixed on the floor, for this was always considered to be the sign of a good doctor. Then, as we reached the designated bed, I looked up for the first time and the sight which greeted me almost made me burst into a fit of uncontrollable laughter. It was, indeed, the vision which I had earlier seen from the other end of the ward, but it was a vision no longer. Her hair was ruffled, her eyes carried more than a hint of imminent tears and, most striking of all, the upper part of her body was now enshrouded in a thick woollen cardigan of navy blue, tightly buttoned at the neck. Her entire appearance was, in fact, more than a little reminiscent of a bundle of clothing left over from a jumble sale.

There were two factors which prevented me from giving vent to my feeling of amusement at the transformation which had taken place. Firstly, I had no wish to add to the humiliation of the poor little thing, for she already exhibited an air of utter despondency. Secondly, and much more significantly, I knew that Sister did not approve of laughter on her ward.

I examined the patient and, needless to say, I could find nothing wrong with her dental condition. I offered up a quiet prayer of thanks to my colleague for his well-justified words of warning. Most of all, however, I realised at that moment that the dangers of War did not all stem from German battleships and dive-bombers.

Captain Lawry appeared to find great difficulty in understanding my lack of enthusiasm for the Wrens' Sick Bay. In truth, this was all part of his act, for he knew only too well that none of my predecessors had tolerated the appointment for any great length of time.

"I'm surprised at you", he said. "Just think of all that beauty laid out for you to admire."

"One can have too much of a good thing, Sir", I replied. "I'm very partial to custard creams, but I wouldn't want them for tea every day."

He took my point, but it seemed that there was nothing he could offer me except the dreary routine of the dockyard surgery. Suddenly, however, his face brightened and he said, "How would you like to look after the Canadians?" The Canadians were a flotilla of destroyers, each bearing the name of a tribe of North American Indians, namely the *Haida, Huron, Athabaskan* and *Iroquois*. They were stationed in the mouth of the Tamar and their job was to harry the German E-boats which were attacking allied convoys sailing up the Channel. They would usually be out for two or three nights, after which they would return to their base to lick their wounds and prepare for the next engagement. I knew that my appointment to the flotilla would call for little work on my part, but at least it would bring me nearer the action, so I accepted with alacrity. Thus it was that, for the next few months, I gave what little time was necessary to the Wrens' Sick Bay but always made sure that I was free when the Canadians came back to port.

I thoroughly enjoyed the comradeship which flowed from those four ships, and I had a particular affection for the *Athabaskan*, where I spent most of my evenings. The captain and I struck up a particularly strong bond of friendship and I was welcomed aboard almost like one of the family. Lieutenant Commander Blythe and his crew all became personal friends, and the hours I spent in their company provided many happy memories which I still cherish.

The bond of friendship which had developed between me and the men of the *Athabaskan* was destined to reach its peak on a certain evening in May 1944. It was, furthermore, an evening which, though beginning in an atmosphere of blissful peace, was to end on a note of high drama. None of us, as we sat chatting over a

HMCS Athabaskan

drink in the wardroom, could have had the slightest inkling of what lay ahead of us in the next few hours. Certainly we had no suspicion of the manner in which the events of that night were destined to affect the lives of each and every one of us.

I had earlier suspected that there might be something different about the evening, for Lt. Cdr. Blythe had made a special point of making sure that I would be going aboard for dinner. He well knew that I never needed much coaxing but, on this occasion, he seemed more than usually persuasive. Any questions which had circulated in my mind, however, had long subsided as we sat around the table in the wardroom to savour the food which the steward laid before us. Then, with the meal consumed and the dishes removed, we lit our cigarettes and passed the port (always to the left, of course). This, for us, was the happy part of the War. Thrown together by the force of circumstance, we would just sit and savour that all-too-brief period of bliss. Our minds became forgetful of the factors which had caused our lives to become entwined and, just for a while, we were at peace.

On this occasion, however, my state of somnolent ecstasy was suddenly disturbed by the fact that the Captain was on his feet with a glass in his hand and, furthermore, that he was making a speech.

Even worse was the realisation that the subject of the speech was me. It was a very flattering speech, though somewhat embarrassing because of its unexpectedness, but it was also mercifully brief. Then, before I could cover my confusion with what I hoped might be a few well-chosen remarks, he informed me that I was to receive a presentation. At this point the steward re-appeared and put into my hands a huge package of duty-free cigarettes. I have no idea how many there were, but certainly there were sufficient to last me for a considerable time, for my consumption was limited to a mere half dozen a day. Anyway, while I was considering this fact, a young seaman entered and presented me with something of far greater value. It was a photograph of the ship's company and it bore the inscription: "To Toothy, with gratitude and thanks from officers and men of HMCS *Athabaskan*". This really was something special and I vowed that, from that moment onward, it would be one of my most treasured possessions and something from which I would never be parted.

Then, the formalities over, we reverted to our usual post-prandial pursuit, just sitting back in lazy relaxation and savouring the mutual pleasure of each other's company. How long our enjoyment lasted on that occasion I cannot recall, but I will never forget the sudden manner in which it came to an end.

It was the strident sound of the alarm siren which roused me from my state of torpor, and then the frantic activity which followed. The entire ship became engulfed in a bustle of sound and motion which contrasted sharply with the tranquil peace which had hitherto surrounded us. The *Athabaskan* had received orders to put to sea.

The sudden transformation of our evening routine was so unexpected that, at first, it was thought that the ship was required to take part in one of the exercises which were occasionally demanded of it. This being so, I suggested to the Captain that perhaps I might be allowed to go along with them, just for the ride. His response was polite but emphatic.

"Exercise be blowed", he said. "There's a pair of German destroyers out there."

The significance of that remark was not lost on me, for it was well known that the German destroyers were much larger and carried far greater fire-power than our Tribal class. They were, indeed, rather more like cruisers, and it was obvious that the Canadians had a bit of a fight on their hands. Thus it was that, to avoid being an encumbrance, I made a hasty exit from the ship.

I had no wish to return to Barracks at that point and I therefore obtained permission to board the *Black Prince*, which was moored nearby. The *Black Prince* was a brand new cruiser, only recently commissioned, which literally bristled with all the latest technology in the way of radar and similar equipment. She would probably have been more than a match for the enemy vessels out in the Channel, but our Lords of the Admiralty had no wish to expose her to the dangers of battle at such an early stage in her career. Thus it was that, for the next few hours, I became a distant witness to the night's activities from the deck of this strange new vessel.

I watched the *Athabaskan* slip her moorings and glide almost silently through the darkness towards the open waters of the Channel. Behind her went the *Huron* and, bringing up the rear, the *Haida*. Then, for what seemed an eternity, there was just darkness and silence. I have little recollection of how long I stood there but, just as I was deciding that I would be well-advised to seek the comfort of my bunk, I became aware of distant flashes lighting up the night sky. This sight, coupled with the muffled rumblings of gunfire, left me in no doubt that the Canadians had engaged the enemy.

The engagement was not a lengthy one, and soon the scene of the operation returned to its earlier aspect of silent darkness. As I sheltered behind the protective security of the *Black Prince*, I had not the slightest conception of what had been taking place out there in those murky waters. It was now just a question of waiting until the Canadians returned to the safety of their home base.

The wait seemed interminable until eventually, just as the first light of dawn began to spread its welcoming rays into the night sky, the unmistakeable form of a destroyer came into view. There was quite a crowd of us on the deck by this time and we could not resist a spontaneous burst of clapping as we identified her as the *Huron*. Then, not many minutes later, the *Haida* followed her up the river, and we strained our eyes into the distance looking for the return of the *Athabaskan*. We waited and waited and, as we peered out into the dawn, we were suddenly hit by the almost unbelievable truth – the *Athabaskan* was not coming back. She had been sunk by enemy shells out there in the dark waters of the Channel. Even worse, her colleagues had been unable to rescue any survivors, and it was well known that the German Navy did not give much time to such niceties.

I will never be able to describe the emotions which assailed me at that fateful moment. I can only say that I was overcome with a feeling of complete numbness from which there seemed to be no escape. That lovely ship, on which I had sat in untroubled peace such a short while before, had gone for ever. Never again would I enjoy the company of those splendid men who had taken her about her business. And never again would I see that photograph which, a few short hours earlier, I had vowed to treasure for the rest of my life. All, all were gone – and to what purpose?

I made my way back to Barracks in the gathering light of dawn and, as I neared that building, I cast my eyes upward. There, hanging limp in the still morning air, was the White Ensign – at half-mast. The news had arrived there before me.

The loss of such a ship was, of course, never publicly announced. It was regarded as highly secret information, in spite of the fact that the enemy had full knowledge of the event. In our close community, however, the news spread like wildfire and it was only a matter of hours before the whole of Devonport knew that the *Athabaskan* had gone. The entire dockyard became clothed in an aura of gloom and despondency which was only lifted when, about a week later, the remaining destroyers levelled the score by sinking one of the German vessels. It was a glaring example of the futility of war, for neither side achieved any lasting gain by either sinking. At the time, however, Devonport rejoiced that the loss of the *Athabaskan* had been avenged.

It might well be thought that the story of my connection with the *Athabaskan* would end at that point, but it was to surface again in a somewhat surprising manner some eighteen months later. By then I was serving with the Patrol Service at Lowestoft and one of my duties was the examination of all personnel entering or leaving the establishment.

On the day in question, I received a telephone call from the Commodore's Office informing me that a rating was being sent to my surgery and that speedy processing was required. The man had been picked up some distance off the coast in an open boat and apparently claimed that he had escaped from a prisoner-of-war camp and was making his way back to England. The story was too far-fetched to be accepted by the authorities, who suspected that he was, in fact, a German spy who had been deliberately planted in the position where he had been found. Thus, he was to be speedily cleared and transported to the Admiralty for interrogation.

The rating duly arrived under a double escort and I proceeded to do what was required of me. It was only as I was going through the examination routine that I became aware of a strange feeling of familiarity. I stood back from the man and said, "Have I come across you before?"

"Yes, Sir", he replied. "Able Seaman Graham, HMCS *Athabaskan*, operating out of Devonport".

Whatever doubts I may have had concerning the existence of some form of supreme destiny dissolved at that very moment. What force other than the hand of Fate could possibly have decreed that his path and mine should cross once again at that fateful moment?

CHAPTER 17
Omaha and Europa

As the spring of 1944 began to give way to early summer, the build-up of forces for the coming assault on Europe reached such proportions that every inch of space in the docks was occupied by ships, with many more lying at anchor in the open water. Particularly conspicuous were the large groups of landing craft waiting to receive their cargoes of men and machines whose destiny lay beyond the far horizon. One such craft was a tank landing ship known simply as L.S.T. 161, and this was a vessel with which I was soon to have a brief association.

The skipper was a former Merchant Navy man who had earlier been called into the Royal Naval Reserve and given the rank of Lieutenant Commander. This trip was to be his last before his release back into civilian life and, as he waited aboard his ship during the final days of May, he decided to put the time to some useful purpose. Thus it was that he presented himself at my surgery with the request that I extract all his remaining teeth. They were 23 in number, and I hardly thought their removal to be the best course of action immediately prior to such a hazardous excursion. He was adamant, however, and the operation was duly carried out over a period of two days. Then followed the customary invitation to share a meal aboard his ship.

To describe her as a ship is really a gross misuse of the word, for she was little more than a dirty old hulk. Clambering aboard her as she lay at anchor in mid-stream was, in itself, somewhat akin to completing a miniature assault course and, once on board, I wondered whether it had been worth the effort. She was a pretty sizeable craft, having room down in the hold for something like two dozen Churchill tanks. Above decks, however, conditions were more than a little cramped. The cook in the tiny galley could just about cope with the baked beans and canned sponge pudding which constituted our meal and, as we ate it, I soon became aware of the necessity for keeping my elbows tucked well into my sides. Fortunately, we were enjoying a spell of glorious weather and we were able to take our drinks outside on the open deck, and it was during this period that Destiny again took a hand in my immediate future.

I learned that L.S.T. 161 had been detailed to make the crossing as part of the back-up for the First U.S. Army in their assault on Omaha Beach, north-west of Bayeux. She was not, however, destined to carry any tanks or troops but, instead, her hold had been filled with bunks to enable her to collect casualties and transport them back to this country. There was just one little detail which had been overlooked in that she was manned solely by her normal crew, with nobody of paramedical status to deal with her eventual human cargo. It was this oversight which gave me the opening and enabled me to coerce my superiors into allowing me to fill the gap.

The choice of Monday, June 5th as D-Day had only been made after consideration of a multitude of factors, not least the question of tides and the state of the moon. The only factor which could not be harnessed to the plan was the weather and when, on the previous day, a violent storm swept in from the west, it seemed that the chance would be lost. By the next day, conditions had deteriorated to such an extent that postponement seemed inevitable and the vast armada of ships, bursting at the seams with men and their armaments, was held fast in ports all along the south coast. Throughout the day the storms persisted, but eventually the Commanders-in-Chief could wait no longer. Tuesday, June 6th was to be D-Day.

Thus, in the early hours of the morning, we slipped our moorings and set forth towards the distant blackness. Even in the confines of the river we were at the mercy of the elements for, with no ballast down below, we were tossed like a cork in the turbulent waters. When we reached the open sea it became much worse. There should have been a moon, but the clouds were so low and threatening that we saw none of its light. The wind came in fierce gusts, whipping up the waves to a height of many feet as we made our way to our first rendezvous. This was at a point south of the Isle of Wight from which the Navy had swept a mine-free channel to the French coast. It was officially designated *Area Z*, but the Navy soon christened it *Piccadilly Circus* for, as the hours went by, 3,000 landing craft and more than 500 warships were destined to move along that route.

A rising, surging sea carried the invasion armada stormily into the night. To the troops who had already been in confinement since embarking on Sunday, the voyage must have seemed interminable. On our floating hulk it was distinctly unpleasant, for we could see nothing of what was going on around us. Cold, stinging spray swept the deck, but it was better up there than down below, where the pitching and throbbing was magnified beyond belief. We plunged on into the night, fortified only by Marmite sandwiches and hot Bovril.

It was only when the first rays of dawn began to lighten the sky that we started to piece together the enormity of the operation in which we were involved. The wheel had turned full circle. Four years earlier, almost to the day, the Royal Navy had rescued the B.E.F. from the beaches of Dunkirk. Now it was bringing them back to fulfil Churchill's promise to the people of Europe.

It was afternoon by the time we reached our destination, and much had taken place before our arrival. Overnight, while R.A.F. Lancasters bombed enemy coastal defences in their concrete emplacements, the heavy guns of the Navy had bombarded them with shellfire from two battleships, two cruisers and a dozen destroyers. At first light they had been given a second dose, this time with the assistance of 300 bombers of the U.S. Air Force. As we approached the scene, it bore all the hallmarks of a massive Naval review. It was impossible to count the number of craft, large and small, which had taken up their pre-arranged stations, but it later transpired that no fewer than 4,000 ships, together with several thousand smaller craft, had crossed the Channel that day.

At one point, as we passed near one of those smaller boats, I heard a shout and saw an arm being waved to attract my attention. I strained my eyes towards the figure and found that it was, indeed, the midshipman with whom I had shared Lady Astor's Cornish pasties a few months earlier. We had unknowingly shared another journey. There was something slightly different about him, however, for he was no longer a middy. Gone were the white flashes on his lapels and on had come the single gold ring which now marked him out as a sub-lieutenant. Even at that distance, it was easy to see his feeling of pride as he took his little craft in towards the beach.

As we rode out the waves, two thoughts were uppermost in our minds. First there was a feeling of admiration at the degree of planning which had gone into the assault, with the result that each individual craft took up its proper station at the appointed time like the movement of pieces in a game of chess. Above all, however, there was the realisation that we were the lucky ones. Not for us

142

No single photograph could convey the magnitude of the invasion fleet which crossed the Channel on D-Day. These two pictures show just a few of the thousands of ships which made the stormy trip.

143

Amphibious DUKWs take to the water while two Tank Landing Ships hover in the background.

had there been the run into the beach and the frantic charge through waist-deep water. It was the troops, most of them weak and nauseated by sickness, cold and wet, who now had to face whatever resistance the enemy might offer. At Omaha, it was the 5th American Corps which suffered most for, by an unlucky chance, they were met by a full-strength German division which, at that very moment, was engaged in an anti-invasion exercise. By the time they were able to force their way inland, the Americans had lost several thousand men and it was some of those who eventually lay in our hold when we made our return journey. We were in sombre mood as we slowly plodded back to Plymouth, and my mind inevitably went back to the carnage I had earlier seen on the streets of London. It all seemed so very pointless.

144

ON DUTY day and night **CALOX** TOOTH POWDER
Flat Tin 13d. Sprinkler Tin 1/10d.

 "WORLD'S LARGEST" EVENING DETAILS

The Evening News

LATE EXTRA

NO. 19,455   LONDON, TUESDAY, JUNE 6, 1944   ONE PENNY

 SENIORS FISH & MEAT PASTES The Best Possible!

Montgomery Leads British, U.S., Canadian Force

WE WIN BEACHHEADS

4,000 Ships, 11,000 Planes in Assault on France: 'All Going to Plan'—Premier

WE LAND IN
JERSEY—Nazis

AN ARMADA OF 4,000 SHIPS, WITH SEVERAL THOUSAND SMALLER CRAFT, ALL BACKED BY 11,000 FRONT-LINE AIRCRAFT, TO-DAY CROSSED THE CHANNEL TO INVADE FRANCE.

Latest reports are that they have established " good beachheads, and are slashing their way inland."

Berlin reported this afternoon that Allied airborne troops had landed on Guernsey and Jersey, in the Channel Islands, where they were " engaged in extremely costly battles."

Shore Batteries Largely Quelled

THE INVASION ARMADA sails across the Channel. Air view on Page Three.

Mr. Churchill, giving the invasion armada figures in the Commons to-day, said: "There are already hopes that actual tactical surprise has been attained, and we hope to furnish the enemy with a succession of surprises during the course of the fight.

" Massed airborne landings have been successfully effected behind enemy's lines. Landings on beaches are proceeding at various points at the present time. The fire of shore batteries has been largely quelled. Obstacles which were constructed in the sea have not proved so difficult as apprehended."

The Anglo-American Allies are sustained by about 11,000 first line aircraft, which can be drawn upon as may be needed for the purposes of battle."

Those hours previously—at 9.01 a.m.—an Allied communiqué gave this official news for which the world has been anxiously waiting.

" Under the command of General Eisenhower, Allied naval forces, supported by strong air forces, began landing Allied armies this morning on the northern coast of France."

As a supplement to this communiqué it was announced that General Montgomery is in command of the Army group carrying out the assault. This Army group includes British, Canadian, and U.S. forces.

Later it was officially revealed that the landings took place in Normandy between 6 a.m. and 8.15 a.m.

German radio gave these points as centre of Allied airborne attack: Barfleur, north-eastern tip of Cherbourg Peninsula; Caretan, or Ome Estuary; north-east of 'Caen, at the north of the Orne Department, between the Seine and the Orne Estuary.

"Paris the Main Objective"

This afternoon Berlin reported that landing barges, under strong air umbrella, are landing near Ouistreham, 16 miles from Caen, that landings were carried out in the Seine Bay area, that it has had been landing in the Arromanches area, 9 miles from Bayeux, and that new aircraft have been made near Marcouf.

The Germans also said our troops were fighting near Caen —10 miles inland. A Berlin correspondent said the Allied objec-tive was Paris, and that they had made landings over an 80-mile front.

A further German report told of a vast Allied airborne landing near St. Vaast de la Hougue, 16 miles south by east of Cherbourg.

Another German report said: " Numerous parachute troops and gliders have been observed in the region of Trouville, just north of Le Havre."

It was learned this afternoon that enemy destroyers and E-boats were reported coming into the operational area. No doubt they are being dealt with.

Reuter's military correspondent states that Hitler is taking personal command of all anti-invasion operations. He is sur-rounded by a Staff, including four Marshals, and is believed to have moved his H.Q. to a place somewhere on Northern France.

His four Marshals are Rundstedt, titular Commander-in-Chief; Rommel, Inspector-General; Sperrle, in charge of Air Forces; and Blaskowitz, acting deputy to Rommel.

At 9.06 a.m. the German radio said: " The combined British-American landing operations against the western coast of Europe from sea and air are stretching over the entire area between Cher-bourg and Le Havre.

MONTY: 'WE SHALL SUCCEED'

GENERAL MONTGOMERY expressed complete confidence in the outcome of the invasion of the Continent in a talk to war correspondents before the attack began.

General Montgomery made these two points, among others:
1.—He expected Rommel to make his greatest fight on the beaches themselves.
2.—The invasion would be a thorough affair, but it would not be impossible to recover later phases of the situation for security reasons.

He warned them that there would be times when it would be impossible to recover later phases of the situation for security reasons.

Allied landing forces " have established some good beach-heads " on the northern coast of France and are slashing their way inland, according to Lieutenant-Colonel C. A. Shoop, who has flown over the scene of the initial thrust.

He expressed surprise at the lack of opposition to our air ground, and naval forces.

" There are lots of burning buildings and bomb craters " he said. " There are burning all over the area "

Colonel Shoop described the Channel as " full of our war-ships," and said there were no German naval vessels about.

The landing by air was particularly impressed with the rigord of the landing operations " Everything seemed to be moving very fast," he said.

Continued on Back Page

ON OTHER PAGES
War Office account of how Invasion was planned.—Page Two.

General Browning's invasion commentary.—Page Two.

Latest news of the Italian cam-paign.—Page Three.

Eye-Witnesses' Stories and other Invasion News on Pages 3 and 4.

A BIRD'S-EYE INVASION VIEW

I SAW THE ARMADA FROM THE AIR

From TOM DOWNES, "Evening News" War Reporter with the R.A.F.

I dawn to-day grim-faced in-fantrymen who for weeks had lain hidden in woods and villages of England, stormed the beaches in Northern France

And the airborne attack was the greatest in history. Thou-sands of British and American parachtroops hurtled out of the big troop - carriers into the French countryside

Gliders carrying more men, guns and transport, cast off from their tug-planes and glided down. Stretched over a vast area, the first of these fell at first light.

In a matter of minutes a com-plete new army went into battle and was ready to strike by the time dawn broke.

From the rail of the vessel in which I crossed the Channel in the first grey hours of dawn I saw the greatest and most amazing armada of ships of all sizes that the world has ever seen.

There were men and men of ships, stretching away until they faded into the haze which made sea and sky merge into a background of blue

Wisps of smoke rose straight from the funnels of the little vessels. Men their bows cleaved the crested waves, rushed the spray into the air, but this turned into a light mist as it was carried by the fresh breeze that blew across the Channel.

No Easy Task

Your task will not be an easy one. Your enemy is well trained, well equipped and battle hardened. He will fight savagely. But this is the year of 1944. Much has happened since the Nazi triumphs of 1940-41.

The United Nations have inflicted upon the Germans great de-feats, in open battle, man to man. Our air offensive has seriously reduced their strength in the air and their capacity to wage war on the ground.

Our home fronts have given us an overwhelming superiority in weapons and munitions of war, and placed at our disposal great reserves of trained fight-ing men. The tide has turned. The free men of the world are marching together to victory.

Full Confidence

I have full confidence in your courage, devotion to duty and skill in battle. We will accept nothing less than full victory.

Good luck, and let us all be-seech the blessing of Almighty God upon this great and noble undertaking.

BEDS FOR WOUNDED
Hospitals Limit Patients

In order to keep beds for wounded needing hospital treat-ment the Ministry of Health announce that hospitals in cer-tain areas are being obliged to limit the number of civilians admitted.

Patients on waiting list who are not on the list urgent nature may be asked to wait.

General de Gaulle has arrived in England, and has had talks with Mr. Churchill and General Eisen-hower.

HIGH-SPIRITED BRITISH ASSAULT TROOPS waiting to board their invasion craft.

BATTLE WILL GROW IN SCALE AND INTENSITY

Premier's Glowing Confidence In Commons Statement To-day

MR. CHURCHILL began his Commons state-ment to-day on the invasion by apolo-gising for his absence earlier. He went on:

The House should, I think, take formal cognisance of the liberation of Rome as the Allied armies under the command of General Alexander, with General Clark, of the United States Services, and General Oliver Leese, in command of the Fifth and Eighth Armies respectively.

I here also to announce to the House that during the night and early dawn of this morning the first of the series of landings in force upon the European Con-tinent has taken place.

In this case the liberating assault fell on the coast of France. An immense armada of upwards of 4,000 ships, together with several thousand smaller craft, crossed the Channel. Mass airborne landings have been successfully effected behind the enemy lines, and landings on the beaches are proceeding at various points at the present time.

The fire of the shore batteries has been largely quelled. The obstacles that were constructed in the sea have not proved so difficult as was apprehended. The Anglo-American Allies are sustained by about 11,000 front-line aircraft, which can be drawn upon as may be needed for the purposes of the battle.

I cannot, of course, commit myself to any particular details. Reports are coming in in rapid succession. So far the commanders who are engaged report that everything is proceeding according to plan. And what a plan!

This vast operation is undoubt-edly the most complicated and diffi-cult that has ever occurred. It involves tides, winds, waves, visibility both from the air and sea standpoint, and the combined employment of land, air and sea forces in the highest degree of intimacy and in contact with con-ditions which could not and cannot be fully foreseen.

There are already hopes that actual tactical surprise has been attained, and we hope to furnish the enemy with a succession of sur-prises during the course of the fighting.

The battle which has now begun will grow constantly in scale and intensity for many weeks to come, and I shall not attempt to speculate upon its course. This I may say—complete unity prevails throughout the Allied armies. There is a brotherhood in arms between us and our friends of the United States.

There is complete confidence in the Supreme Commander, General Eisenhower, and his lieutenants, and also in the Commander of the Expeditionary Force.

They are hitting any target that has a bearing on the strength of the German Army at the front. They fly literally into the mouths of guns and dive within half the spans which hold bridges to-gether.

Weapons of Humphreys

Ten times, right up to zenith, 100 or more heavy bombers went over, pounding up the German guns.

I can now reveal that Bomber Command began to attack these and other batteries along the coast of France almost a month ago.

Turn to Back Page

PONTINGS

'LIQUID STOCKINGS'
Well applied in the legs gives the perfect finish of sheer silk stockings. Waterproof and sun proof. Large box Bottle 3/6
Post and Packing 3d.

Handsome!
ALL-WOOL COAT
9 gns

SAMPLE GLOVES
A Maker's Collection
8/-

OUTSIZE FROCK
£4.9.9

LEG TAN

PONTINGS The House for Value KENSINGTON W8

BLACKOUT 10.47 p.m. to 5.6 a.m.
Moon rises 5.45 a.m. Moon sets 6.51 a.m.

Our feeling as we tied up at our mooring in the Tamar was one of distinct anti-climax, relieved only by the arrival of a couple of Wrens in a little liberty boat bringing us refreshment. I forget the exact nature of the meal, but I well recall that we finished with strawberries and cream. We felt a strange mixture of emotions as we sat on that dirty old hulk eating our repast and knowing that, not many miles away, vast armies of men were locked in mortal combat. Even now, after so many years, the sight of the first strawberries of summer unfailingly brings back memories of the day when Britain and her allies set out to liberate the peoples of Europe.

Within a week I was again off on my travels, and this time it was to a very welcoming destination, for it was only just outside my home county. It was, in fact, to HMS *Europa* at Lowestoft, the headquarters of the Royal Naval Patrol Service.

The main centre of activity there was the dock area, from which minesweepers and motor torpedo boats set forth to carry out their duties in the coastal waters. It was, in fact, the minesweepers which had brought me there, for most of them were converted trawlers, manned in many cases by the same local fishermen who, in more peaceful times, had sailed out in them to bring back the rich harvest of the seas. The toothy who had preceded me in the post had been unable to strike up any sort of relationship with those strange men and their even stranger manner of speech. In my case, however, things were very different. I had spent most of my life in the Norfolk countryside and they immediately accepted me as one of them. We spoke the same language and, above all, we knew each other's ways.

It was not only in the docks, however, that the Navy was in evidence, for there was hardly any part of the town which was unaffected by its presence. The Sparrows' Nest, formerly a local place of entertainment, had become the main centre of administration, whilst such places as St. Luke's Hospital and the Brewery had also been taken over. Ratings were billeted in private homes all over the area whilst a group of houses on Gunton Cliff was home for most of the officers. The most palatial of these was Briar Clyffe which, as our wardroom, was the centre of our social life. A few of the more senior officers lived in the upper rooms, but my sleeping quarters were next door in a rather more modest building known simply as Number 9.

The palatial sleeping quarters which I shared with a cabinmate at Number 9.
The two pictures above my cot are of Deanna Durbin and Patricia Roc.

Dental colleagues at HMS Europa. From the left, Surgeon Lieutenants Peter Reed,
Bob Bagshaw, Jeff Rutledge, Alan Rossiter and Maurice Widdup.

147

The Dental Department was situated in a pair of houses in Royal Avenue, and it was there that I was once again destined to team up with David Simpson. Our paths had not crossed since our days at Devonport, but we were soon back in partnership in more ways than one. We occupied adjoining surgeries and, apart from social advantages, this also led to a joint business venture. Precious metals were in very short supply and such items as wedding rings were by no means up to peacetime standards. We could get hold of gold and silver for dental purposes, however, and, when we were asked by a colleague to produce a ring for his forthcoming marriage, we had no problem in obtaining the necessary raw materials. Once we had produced our first satisfactory specimen, orders came in from a steadily-increasing clientele and we soon had a flourishing business. Before long we had diversified into such things as silver brooches bearing the Naval crest and precious metal castings of various insects which we first anaesthetised with the ethyl chloride spray normally used for inducing numbness in our patients' gums.

At the time, our Senior Dental Officer was a Surgeon Commander who had passed the normal peacetime retirement age and who was content to let life slip by without unduly bothering the rest of us. He rarely showed his face in our surgeries and it was many years since he had engaged in active dentistry. It came as something of a shock, therefore, when he suddenly announced that he proposed to do an extraction for an unsuspecting sailor. Even worse was the fact that, as David was on leave, his surgery was to be the scene of the operation. David had given me the key to his cabinet so that I could carry on the business in his absence and, when the Commander asked me for it, I feared that our nefarious activity would be discovered. I had no alternative other than to hand it over, however, and I watched as he opened the door and studied the contents. There, neatly arranged, were the rings and brooches, the little plaster moulds and the supplies of gold and silver. The Commander took it all in and then, looking over the top of his spectacles, turned towards me.

"He's always making some ruddy thing", he said. "But you can't say anything to him – he's such a nice chap."

I breathed a sigh of relief.

Before long, the Commander was finally put out to grass and a new one arrived. He was a tall man, upright and unbending, and he wore his cap in such a manner that he immediately became known as "The Stationmaster". One of his first actions was to appoint me as his deputy, which normally would have meant promotion. Unfortunately, the rules decreed that no surgeon lieutenant could achieve higher rank until he had either completed six years' service or had reached the age of thirty. The fact that I had achieved neither of these meant that I was to complete the remainder of my Naval career as an acting lieutenant-commander with nothing to show for it. It did bring certain advantages, however, for the fact that he had connections in Saxmundham meant that his periods of absence tended to become somewhat frequent.

He also instituted the weekly routine of Commander's Rounds, during which he would carry out a meticulous inspection of our surgeries. This was mainly to keep our sick berth attendants on their toes, for the cleanliness of the premises was their responsibility. My S.B.A. was a young lad named Jack Kemp who was little more than a schoolboy and who had attached himself to me with all the devotion of a faithful spaniel. He worked hard and long to ensure that my surgery would meet with approval and, when the Commander arrived, he stood transfixed to await the outcome. The inspection was long and thorough – a white handkerchief on the end of a stick would reveal the slightest trace of dust in odd corners and a long-handled mirror would similarly expose any degree of neglect in other less-accessible places. Only on very rare occasions did the Commander express complete satisfaction.

Young Kemp was always eager to achieve perfection and, after the first of the weekly rounds, he asked me for advice as to how he might best satisfy the Commander.

"You've done everything humanly possible", I said, "but I would suggest that you look around at all the exposed ledges and see if you can find a coin on one of them."

He looked at me with a puzzled expression on his face until I explained that it was an old trick which was employed throughout the Service. The Commander would place a penny on some out-of-the-way surface and, if it was still there when he did his next inspection, he immediately knew that no duster or brush had disturbed the area since his last visit. Kemp climbed on a chair to have a look and, sure enough, right in the corner of the picture rail which ran round the walls of the room lay a single penny.

"What shall I do with it?" he asked.

"Take it away and put two ha'pennies in its place", I said.

It was an old dodge which I had learned at Devonport, and it

The author, and S.B.A. Jack Kemp, who tried so hard to please.

never failed. Sure enough, when the Commander carried out his next inspection, he climbed up and felt along the picture rail. There he found the two little coins replacing the one he had left and he knew that the rail had been cleaned. He also knew who was responsible for the switch of coins, for he was well aware that Kemp would never have had the nerve to do it. He looked down at me with a huge grin on his face and I swear that I detected just a suggestion of a sly wink.

There was one other occasion on which I was able to put one over on the Commander and it began during a game of snooker. I never enjoyed playing against him for not only did he have little talent for the game but he also found it difficult to accept defeat with any degree of grace. Thus, I had to try and play even more badly than him in order that he might win, and our games tended to be rather lengthy affairs in which conversation frequently played a major part. On the day in question we were discussing psychosomatic pain. This is a condition in which pain occurs for purely psychological reasons rather than from any physical cause, and it was particularly relevant to teeth.

I had come across a number of cases in which men whose wives were pregnant developed toothache for no apparent reason. The pain, though psychological in origin, was nevertheless severe and was by no means imaginary. Furthermore, extraction of the offending tooth served no useful purpose, for the pain would then transfer itself to the next one. Relief would not come until the end of the wife's pregnancy, when all symptoms would magically disappear. When I had first encountered the condition I had tended to regard it with scepticism, but I had later seen it with such frequency, particularly among countryfolk, that I knew it to be a true condition. The Commander's reaction was predictable.

"Poppycock", he said. "I've never heard such a load of rubbish", and he made it plain that he considered the matter closed.

Some weeks later he developed raging toothache in an upper wisdom and he called upon me to extract it for him. I had a good look at the tooth and could find no reason why it should give him such discomfort. It was then that, without thinking of the consequences and purely in jocular vein, I suggested that his wife might possibly be pregnant.

"As a matter of fact, she is", he replied. "But it's nothing to do with that. I'm not one of your country yokels. I know when I've got toothache." And he insisted that I extract it.

The next day the pain was still there, transferred to the adjacent tooth, and it continued until, a couple of weeks later, his wife presented him with a son. Then it miraculously disappeared. Even then, however, he would not admit that it was in any way connected with his wife's condition. It was purely coincidence!

CHAPTER 18

The End of the Storm

I suppose it was inevitable that, amongst the seething mass of people who constituted the workforce at HMS *Europa*, there should be a wide diversity of talents of every kind. Every conceivable trade and profession was represented and we were particularly well-served in the way of entertainment. We had in our midst a number of famous names from both the world of variety and the legitimate stage, together with the professional musicians who got together to form the Blue Mariners Dance Band. Their fame spread far and wide for, quite apart from their local performances, they made regular trips to London to do a series of weekly broadcasts for the B.B.C.

Sometimes, however, talent revealed itself in the most unexpected of places and it became my good fortune to discover one such example. I was examining a group of seamen who were being sent on a foreign draft and, as so often happened at such times, there was one amongst them who did not want to go. One became accustomed to hearing all sorts of fabricated tales as to why a complainant wished to dodge such a draft and it was necessary to adopt a certain hardness of heart to avoid being hoodwinked. In this particular case, however, I became aware of a distinct feeling of sincerity in the rating's manner and I listened to his story.

His name was Austin and he came from London, where his parents ran a small shoe-manufacturing concern. His father, however, had fallen ill and his mother was struggling to prevent the collapse of the business. While stationed at Lowestoft, Austin could dash up to London now and again to keep an eye on things, but a foreign posting would, of course, make that impossible. I believed his story and I am pleased to say that my faith in human nature was not misplaced. I stopped his draft and took him on my staff as a messenger.

The following morning, when he reported for duty, he showered me with gratitude and expressed the wish that he might be allowed to show his appreciation in tangible form by drawing a picture of me. I had never regarded myself as an artist's model, but his

The author as portrayed by Seaman Austin.

153

persuasiveness was such that I agreed. The sitting lasted no more than two minutes, after which he told me that he would bring me the finished picture the next day. He was as good as his word and the following morning he, in fact, presented me with two drawings. One could not really call them portraits, for they were rather more in the form of caricatures. I was, however, completely taken aback by the talent which he possessed and the two pictures immediately became prized possessions. Before long, Seaman Austin was busily engaged in painting murals in messes and other buildings throughout the establishment.

The officers in the wardroom came from a wide variety of professions and, though some of them were not engaged in their peacetime callings whilst in the Service, there were times when their talents proved extremely useful. In particular, we had a solicitor and a barrister whose services came well to the fore when two of our colleagues had a slight brush with authority.

The two men in question were young medical officers who habitually spent every evening drinking themselves into varying stages of intoxication. Sometimes this happened in the Mess, but more frequently they would cycle to a hostelry a mile or two up the coast to engage in their roistering. Then, at closing time, they would pedal ponderously back and collapse into their bunks. It was something of a mystery to the rest of us that they unfailingly came down to breakfast the next morning in a state of complete sobriety.

The trouble was that they never carried lights on their bicycles, and this information became known to a member of the local constabulary who decided to put a stop to such flagrant law-breaking. Thus it was that, one night as they rode their machines through the gates of Briar Clyffe, he was waiting in the shrubbery to apprehend them. The summonses were duly served, calling upon the miscreants to present themselves at the local Magistrates' Court on a charge of riding without lights. Of course, the obvious course of action would have been to plead guilty and pay the standard five-shilling fine. This, however, would have been a blot on the Navy's escutcheon and a Mess meeting was called to discuss the matter. The barrister and the solicitor put their heads together and eventually they came up with the solution. It was their considered opinion that, by standing within the grounds of Briar Clyffe when he made the arrests, the police constable was, in fact, guilty of trespassing on Admiralty property. Thus, there could be no case to answer. Accordingly, it was decided that the charges would be contested, and it was even suggested that a counter-charge of trespass might be brought against the Police.

In due course, on the appointed day, the two accused presented themselves at the Court, together with their defending solicitor and barrister. That was not all, however, for about a score of us went along with them to observe the proceedings from the public gallery. The Magistrates were somewhat taken aback by this course of events. In the first place, they had obviously expected the usual plea of guilty. The fact that the accused were being represented by learned counsel on such a trivial charge created an obvious feeling of amazement, and the sight of those solid rows of Naval uniforms packed tightly in the public gallery added to their discomfiture. They consulted together and announced their decision that the defence plea would be accepted and that there was no case to answer. Our counter-charge against the Police was not proceeded with, for the honour of the Service had been vindicated. We left the Courtroom in high spirits.

That night, a celebration took place in the wardroom. The gin flowed and the two doctors drank themselves into a state of near-unconsciousness. Then, with full ceremony, they were carried upstairs and tucked into their respective bunks, where they fell asleep like innocent babes.

It is doubtful whether the entire strength of the legal profession could have saved a certain lieutenant when he faced a court martial on a charge of "conduct unbecoming an officer". His crime was basically that of having entertained a Wren on board his ship and, although that sort of thing was by no means a rare occurrence, it was nevertheless an offence in the eyes of the Service. It was his great misfortune that the assignation was discovered and he found himself appearing before his senior officers.

He was a very pleasant chap who, though based in the docks, was a friend of many of us at Briar Clyffe. The Wren was also not unknown to us, at least by reputation. The daughter of a country parson, she had received a somewhat sheltered upbringing and, on joining the Service, had found the unaccustomed freedom from parental restriction rather to her liking. Thus, if ever there was a party or celebration of any kind, she was certain to be there.

The evening in question had begun innocently enough with a candlelit dinner and a bottle of wine on board the little ship. As time went on, however, the lieutenant imbibed somewhat too freely and, being overcome with tiredness, laid back on his bunk and fell fast asleep. The girl, though not in such an intoxicated condition, could not prevent herself from developing a degree of hysteria, and it was the sound of her screams, falling upon the ears of Naval police patrolling the dockside, which brought about the officer's downfall.

Things might not have been too bad if certain sections of the national Press had not got hold of the story and proceeded to give the case their fullest attention. We were deeply offended by the fact that, though the officer's name was freely quoted, that of the Wren was never made public. Thus, the more lurid of the Sunday newspapers carried banner headlines about the scandal of the Naval Officer and "Wren X". It soon reached the stage when any Wren going on leave from *Europa* knew full well that the first thing she would hear on arriving at her destination would be, "Ah, you must be Wren X".

The lieutenant was, of course, found guilty. Accordingly, he was dismissed his ship and reduced to the rank of sub-lieutenant. The Wren was transferred to another establishment where, by a stroke of genius on somebody's part, she was billeted at a vicarage.

It was during my spell of duty with the Patrol Service that my life was given a new dimension by the acquisition of my first motor car. It was a 1936 Morris Eight two-seater tourer and it belonged to a petty officer who was due to leave the depot for an overseas posting. We met one evening for a trial run and my first few minutes at the wheel signalled the start of a long-lasting love affair between that splendid car and me. I simply had to possess her.

There was, however, one snag which threatened to prevent any possible transaction, and that was the financial aspect. The asking price was £170 and my total assets at the bank amounted to a mere £172. 4s. 2d. I could afford to buy the car, but I would then be unable to meet the charge of £9. 19s. 6d. which I had been quoted for a year's insurance. I thus embarked on my first-ever bit of bargaining, fearing all the time that any degree of intransigence on my part might prevent me from acquiring the object of my affections. Eventually we agreed on a figure of £160, together with the promise that he would put two gallons of petrol into the tank at no extra cost.

My future wife was a Wren at Lowestoft at the time and we decided that the new acquisition was too lovely a creation to be

156

My wife stands proudly beside Jeannie, our much-loved 1936 Morris 8. At the rear is my mother, with my father's saloon version of the same car.

known simply as "the car". Thus, for reasons which escape me, we christened her Jeannie and, for the next six or seven years, she was destined to carry us many thousands of miles over vast areas of the country. It was only the impending arrival of a son, some years later, which reluctantly caused us to part with her in favour of a model more in keeping with the mature state of parenthood. No other car, however, has ever approached the position which Jeannie unfailingly held in our affections.

Even so, I cannot honestly claim that Jeannie always provided us with trouble-free motoring, for she was inclined to have her little idiosyncracies. We soon learned how to cope with them, however, and when the petrol pump occasionally refused to function it only needed a sharp tap with a wrench to get it going again. Then, when the frayed brake cables got tangled up in the drums and brought the car to a grinding halt, it was only a matter of waiting for the brake drums to cool down and all would be well. I suppose her most alarming trick was on the two occasions when the ball and socket joints at the ends of the track rods parted company and Jeannie careered uncontrollably across the road. Even this fault, however, was easily remedied and we were ever ready to forgive her for her little failings.

157

It was Jeannie, indeed, who was to take me on the next part of my travels when I eventually left Lowestoft. On May 4th 1945 the German forces had surrendered and four days later the War in Europe was over. The people of Britain danced in the streets and we at Briar Clyffe had our own modest celebration with a mid-morning issue of rum. Then, on August 9th, an atom bomb was dropped on Hiroshima, followed by another one on the city of Nagasaki. The Japanese capitulated and the whole world began to count the cost of the six years of carnage which had mercifully come to an end.

Any thoughts which the average serviceman may have had of a speedy release back into civilian life were soon shattered for, with such vast numbers of men and women under arms, demobilisation was to be a slow and lengthy process. In my own case, it was to be a further twelve months before I could finally lay aside my uniform.

For several months after VJ-Day we engaged in a steady scaling down of operations at *Europa* and then, packing my belongings into the back of my little car, I made my way south to HMS *Victory* at Portsmouth. My stay there was not destined to be a lengthy one, but it was of sufficient duration to leave me with a host of memories in a wide variety of forms.

There was the thrill of playing football for Portsmouth at Fratton Park and the joy of discovering the delights of that lovely little bit of England at Selsey Bill. Then, of course, there was the Band of the Royal Marines. There is no sound in the world to compare with that of "The Band" and, as we marched behind them on our weekly Church Parade, we held ourselves ten feet tall. The buglers announced the start of every day when, at sunrise, the White Ensign was ceremonially raised, and they repeated the procedure when the colours were later laid to rest for the night. On special occasions the full band treated us to the splendour of the Sunset Ceremony with its mixture of bugle calls, hymns and the 23rd psalm. If I was ever unfortunate enough to be wrecked on a desert island, that would be the one record which I would wish to have with me.

Of all my memories of Portsmouth, however, the one which I recall with greatest pleasure is that of sitting on the top of Portsdown Hill and looking at the city spread out below. During my time at HMS *Victory*, the Wren who was later to share my life came down on leave and stayed with relatives in Southsea. In the

*The Band of Her Majesty's Royal Marines on ceremonial parade
alongside HMS Victory.*

evenings, as dusk began to fall, we would drive up the hill and, eating fish and chips out of newspaper, would watch the lights coming on in the distant buildings. I think it was those lights, after so many years of darkness, which finally convinced us that the War really was over.

I would have been quite content to complete my time in the Service at Portsmouth, but Fate decreed otherwise when a signal suddenly arrived informing me of my next posting. Furthermore, it was not just a feeling of disappointment which I experienced as I read the signal. It hit me, indeed, with the force of a thunderbolt, for I was required to report aboard a certain ship at Simonstown, on the South Atlantic Station. Earlier in my Service career, I would have regarded such an appointment with a high degree of pleasure. Now, however, with my time for demobilisation only a few months away, I was by no means keen on the prospect of spending two years in that distant South African port.

Fortunately for me, it proved to be a mistake, for the appointment should have gone to a toothy who was making the Navy his career. I breathed again, but I still had to move from Pompey. My new destination was not long in being revealed to me and, when it came, it couldn't have been a greater contrast from Simonstown. It was, in fact, to the Royal Naval Camp at Stockheath.

CHAPTER 19
The Lost Legion

I had never heard of Stockheath and I had been unable to locate it on any map, but I was told that it was a tiny village just outside Havant. This was familiar territory to me, so I was confident that I would have little difficulty in finding the camp. I simply needed to get to Havant and then ask for directions from some local resident. Thus, I loaded my belongings into my car and set off in confident mood.

On arriving in Havant I stopped the first person I saw and asked him the way to Stockheath, but he had never heard of the place. I repeated my request to another man with a similar result. By the time I had repeated my question to six people I had begun to think I was on some kind of mystery tour for, while the first five claimed that no such place existed, even the last one had been able to do no more than wave his arm vaguely out into the distance and say, "It's somewhere over there".

It was then that I decided to use my instinct and simply go and look for the place. An hour later I was still looking, and I had driven up and down the same roads so many times that the entire area had now become familiar to me. The trouble was that, as I scanned the horizon, there was not the slightest sign of any kind of human existence. There was no house, no church, no farm building of any kind – not even as much as a single cow in a field. Then, just as I was on the brink of admitting defeat, I noticed a narrow, winding lane leading apparently to nowhere in particular. It looked completely unpromising, but I decided to give it a try.

Half a mile down this track I was beginning to doubt the wisdom of my action when suddenly, near a gap in the hedgerow, I spotted a strange structure which was vaguely reminiscent of the outside lavatories which, in earlier years, had been a familiar feature of the countryside. I slowly approached the peculiar little edifice and, as I drew nearer, the truth gradually dawned upon me – it was a sentry box. That was not all, however, for, as I brought my car to a halt, I could see that it was, in fact, occupied. There, on the floor, was a seaman, crouched in a posture of somnolent unconsciousness with a rifle, complete with bayonet, lying casually across his lap. I suppose it was the sound of my brakes which roused him from his slumbers. Whatever it was, he struggled clumsily to his feet, almost dropping his rifle as he did so. I could well imagine the state of turmoil which existed in his mind at that moment for, not only had he been guilty of sleeping on duty, but he would now have to decide what kind of salute to give me. An officer of my rank was entitled simply to a butt salute, which involved holding the rifle over the left shoulder and giving the butt a sharp tap with the right hand. In the case of a more senior officer, however, it was a question of "presenting arms", a much more intricate manoeuvre in which the rifle was held in front of one's body and more or less offered to the officer in question. The poor man's mind was in such a state of chaos, however, that he proceeded to acknowledge my presence with a jumbled mixture of both salutes, with a few other unusual manipulations thrown in for good measure. The result was a spectacle which gave the distinct impression of having been carried out by an intoxicated juggler, and it was only by the grace of God that he escaped stabbing himself with his own bayonet. I told him to "stand easy", but he was not in a sufficiently stable condition to carry out even that simple command. Accordingly, having obtained from him the information that this was, indeed, Stockheath Camp, I drove through the gap and started off along the track which lay ahead.

At first, all I could see was a distant area of dense woodland but, as I got nearer, I could make out the shape of countless Nissen huts hidden among the trees. At that point, my main concern was to make sure where the quarterdeck was, for this was the holy of holies and to have driven my car across it would have brought down upon me the combined wrath of every one of our Lords of the Admiralty. Accordingly, I brought the car to a halt some twenty yards short of the spot where the White Ensign was flying and, seeing the figure of an officer, I hailed him as loudly as I could.

"I'm coming aboard", I yelled in true Naval fashion. "Where can I put my car?"

"Bring it down here", came back the voice.

"Where's the quarterdeck?" I queried.

"Quarterdeck?" said the voice. "We don't bother about things like that here. Just drive straight through."

I couldn't believe my ears, for back at *Victory* I would have been shot for committing such a crime. I took him at his word, however,

162

and it was not long before I realised that this was simply the first of many revelations which were to make Stockheath the strangest establishment I had ever encountered. Little wonder, I thought, that the Admiralty had never bothered to give it the fictitious name of HMS Something-or-other! It just didn't deserve it!

I was given a warm welcome aboard and was soon being regaled with the history of the place. It had been built, I was told, at the start of the War in order to house the many workers who would be needed in the dockyard at Portsmouth. Upon its completion, they had sent a deputation to inspect it and had immediately declared it to be unfit for human habitation. Thus, it had been handed over to the Navy, who had retained possession of it ever since.

It covered a vast area and, in the earlier years of the War, it had provided accommodation for more than a thousand ratings, together with some two hundred officers. It had been admirably sited from the point of view of camouflage for, being completely hidden away under massive trees, it was as difficult to find from the air as I had found it to be from the land. By the time I arrived, the number of personnel had dwindled considerably and only a tiny portion of the camp was being used. There appeared to be about two dozen officers and a literally unknown number of ratings. Strangest of all was the fact that not one of the men at Stockheath knew why he had been sent there. There was one lieutenant who had been listed as missing when the *Prince of Wales* had been sunk in 1941. He was happily drawing his pay and his only worry was that he might be overlooked when his time came for demobilisation. We even had a Fleet Air Arm pilot, known to everybody simply as "Wings", who hadn't been near a plane for over a year.

My job was well-defined, for I was appointed as Senior Dental Officer to Stockheath and two other nearby camps. The post was not as demanding as I had expected, however, for the number of patients I was destined to treat at Stockheath could have been numbered on the fingers of one pair of hands, and I never even found the other camps. This was rather a pity, for the Dental Department was one of the finest I ever encountered in the Service. Similarly, the single medical officer had the use of a Sick Bay which was lavish in the extreme, but even he led a life of enforced idleness.

My first introduction to my fellow officers came before lunch on that first day. It was not my normal practice to frequent the bar at such times, partly out of respect for my mess bill and partly because the imbibing of alcohol at that time of day tended to have a soporific effect which left me in no fit state to face the afternoon. On the first day, however, it was the best way of getting to know one's companions, so I considered it a forgiveable luxury.

It was as I stood, glass in hand, talking to a group of the others that, from behind me, I suddenly heard a voice in the broadest of Norfolk accents accosting me with, "Hey, bor. Dew your father keep a dickey?"

"Blast, no", I replied in similar tones. "But he ha' got a hoss and he want a fule to ride it. How about you?"

Then, turning round, I almost froze with horror as I realised that the man with whom I had been engaged in that little bit of banter was the Commander. He was all smiles, however, for he also hailed from Norfolk and had obviously discovered my origins before I arrived. We thus struck up a pleasing relationship right from the start, a fact which was always gratifying on joining a new ship.

By the time I sought the sanctuary of my bunk on that first night, my mind was desperately trying to come to terms with all the peculiarities of that strange establishment and its lost legion of inhabitants. What I did not realise at that moment, however, was that those first few hours had been merely a prelude to a vastly greater wealth of oddities which were still to be revealed to me.

I was just in that pleasant state of somnolence which precedes full sleep when I was suddenly brought back to consciousness by a rapid succession of thudding noises outside. It gave the distinct impression of being the sound of galloping horses, charging around in gay abandon. I shot up into a sitting position to determine the source of the strange noise, but it had stopped as quickly as it had started. I lay down again and then, just as I was dozing pleasantly towards sleep, the sound was suddenly repeated. Was it really horses' hooves, or was it just a creation of my troubled mind? I was frantically trying to solve the mystery of this strange phenomenon when, suddenly, all was revealed to me for, looking up, I could see a horse's head peering down at me from my open window. I must confess that, at that moment, I had grave doubts concerning my sanity.

It later transpired that the horses belonged to our Commanding Officer, a certain Captain Villiers, who allowed them to range freely through the camp. I was not even aware that we merited an officer of such high seniority, but it mattered little, for he spent little time with us. He held a senior position in the horse racing world, being the starter at many of the big meetings, and thus we rarely saw him.

While the Sick Bay and my own department were of the highest order, the same could not be said of our living quarters. The actual Mess was not too bad, bearing in mind the fact that it was little more than a glorified Nissen hut. It was clean and warm, and we were able to eat and relax with a reasonable degree of comfort. Our individual quarters, however, were such a complete and utter disgrace that any Public Health Inspector would have been stricken down with apoplexy at the mere sight of them.

Each small hut was partitioned off into four parts so that we all had our individual cabins. They were small and cramped, but this gave us little cause for concern. What really bothered us was the fact that they were both dark and damp. No ray of sunlight ever penetrated the overhead canopy of trees and very little air circulated beneath. The result was that any clothing laid out for use the next day would, by the morning, be almost wringing wet. It was a complete mystery that the Sick Bay was not permanently full of pneumonia cases. It is true that each cabin had its own heating system in the form of a tortoise stove. The only trouble was that nobody had ever thought to provide fuel for these contraptions and the best we could manage was fallen twigs from the trees. We tried our hardest, but such fuel doesn't last long on a tortoise stove.

Over a period of time, a tradition had been developed which decreed that Friday night was always "burn-up night". We would all then make a concerted effort to inject a little warmth into the area by gathering sticks from the trees, filling our stoves and lighting them. Then it was a question of dashing out to gather more supplies before the first lot burnt out. The stoves were very uncooperative, however, and, with one big rush of flame, each bundle of gleanings went up in smoke in a matter of seconds. It was always a hopeless task and the best we ever achieved was a few minutes of flickering flame accompanied by a flimsy wisp of smoke ascending the chimney.

Then, one day, the problem was solved, at least for Wings and me. He had been out exploring the distant reaches of the camp where no human foot had trod for years and he had come upon a hoard of coal.

"There's a huge pile of the stuff", he said. "There must be tons".

165

The only snag was that this precious find was, in his estimation, a mile and a half away.

"That's all very well", I said, "but how on earth can we get it over here?"

He looked at me with a quizzical expression on his face.

"I thought perhaps we might get it in the back of your car".

The very suggestion horrified me. The idea of carting coal in my precious little car appalled me. The temptation, however, was too great to be resisted and, after four or five trips, we must have shifted about half a ton. There only remained one other problem. If we had stacked it near the huts the other chaps would have pinched it and it wouldn't last long among twenty of us. The only solution was to pile it up against the wall inside our cabins, and that is what we did. Climbing over it to get into bed was a bit of a hazard, but that was a mere detail.

That night was burn-up night, and Wings and I lit our fires and filled the stoves with coal. The flames spread their warmth through our cabins whilst, up on the roof, our twin chimneys billowed great columns of smoke up through the trees. Outside, our colleagues were charging madly about gleaning twigs in the usual vain effort to conjure up some semblance of fire. Wings and I sat on the step outside the hut quietly smoking our pipes and secretly gloating. The other chaps were mystified, but we were answering no questions. We kept our little secret to the bitter end.

In spite of its many peculiarities, Stockheath did at least try to retain a semblance of what was known as "Big Ship Routine". Thus, the early morning air would be shattered by the sound of the bosun's pipe echoing over the tannoy system, followed by the call of "Hands to Divisions". The divisional officers would then head for the parade ground and wait for the ratings to present themselves for inspection. No ratings ever arrived, however, for, knowing that the call would come at a set hour, they had already disappeared up the hill and into the protective cover of the woods. There they would play cards and engage in other trivial pursuits until, a few hours later, the bosun's pipe would herald the call of "Hands to Dinner". Only then would they re-emerge and take up their places in the day's routine.

Even the departure of any form of motorised transport from the camp was carried out in accordance with the traditions of the Service and, whatever its form, it was always known as a boat.

Thus, even the pick-up truck which went down into Havant to collect a supply of fresh vegetables was sent on its way with the sound of the pipe and the call of "Away Ship's Boat".

Boredom was, of course, the main hazard at Stockheath and I found various ways of combating it. On one sunny afternoon I decided to take a drive over to Hayling Island and spend a few hours on the beach, and it proved so pleasing that I decided to repeat it. The only snag was that, though Service vehicles were allowed free access, I was required to pay a toll for my car to cross to the island. I soon overcame this anomaly by organising beach parties and making use of one of the camp vehicles. Thus, twenty or thirty of us would pack into one of the trucks and head off for an afternoon on the beach.

I also occupied much of my time in writing. I was, at the time, engaged in preparing a series of books on nature subjects for a firm of publishers in London. Then they asked me to write another book concerned with "Dentistry as a Career". This was duly completed but, within a week or two, the firm went into bankruptcy. Fortunately, they sent me my cheque before they fell into this parlous state but, though the book was produced, I never saw it.

Another activity which occupied a certain amount of my time began when the Commander announced my appointment as Mess Secretary and Catering Officer. It was something I had not previously encountered, but I threw myself into the post with something approaching gay abandon. I approved the menus which the Petty Officer Steward prepared and I made frequent trips into Havant to bring back such things as fruit, vegetables and provisions. One of the more demanding aspects of my task, however, was that of preparing my fellow-officers' mess bills and, more to the point, making sure they paid them.

In order that I might start off on a sound footing I decided to make a thorough study of the accounts book which had been kept by my predecessor prior to his departure from Stockheath. It was then that the first crisis presented itself, for I immediately found that there was a deficit of several hundred pounds. The reason for this was not difficult to find for, on combing through the figures, I found a total of some twenty or thirty accounts against which there was no record of payment having been received. I refused to accept this state of affairs and, accordingly, I traced the whereabouts of most of the debtors and sent each one a reminder and a request for settlement. Then it was merely a question of sitting back and waiting for the cheques to come rolling in.

I had only a short time to wait for, within a few days, a large pile of envelopes awaited me as I entered the Mess for breakfast. The immediate response to my letters had been far greater than I had expected and I experienced a glow of satisfaction at the thought that I could, at least, go some way towards balancing the books. It was only when I opened the first envelope that a tiny suggestion of doubt entered my mind. As I nervously worked through the pile, that feeling of doubt gradually grew stronger. By the time I had reached the final one I was in utter despair, for each letter, though couched in differing terms, bore the same message. Some carried strongly worded references to my lack of ability as a mess secretary whilst, at the other end of the scale, there were thinly-veiled threats of libel action. The one thing which they all had in common was that each writer claimed that his bill had been paid and, furthermore, offered tangible evidence in support of that fact.

I consulted the Comnmander and, acting upon his instructions, burnt the book and started on a new one.

CHAPTER 20

The Party's Over

The last few weeks of my Naval career were destined to pass by at little more than walking pace, for that was how everything was done at Stockheath. Day followed day in a mainly undisturbed rhythm and the only real excitement came whenever the latest rumour about demobilisation filtered through. Since the end of the War we had been living our lives in an atmosphere of anticlimax and most of us were impatient to get out into the wonderful new world which we had been promised. For all our impatience, there was nothing we could do to speed things up so, as those warm days of July slipped away, we just went through the pretence of still being sailors. In such a place as Stockheath pretending was no problem.

There were just two little incidents which came along near the end to add a little touch of variety to our lives. Both were so sudden and unexpected that, just for a while, they transformed our little settlement from its normal state of inertia into a veritable ant-heap of activity. Both, furthermore, succeeded in being nothing more than a complete waste of time and energy.

The first upheaval occurred one sunny afternoon as I was chatting with a small group of other officers outside the First Lieutenant's Office. We saw a seaman emerge from the administrative block not many yards away, but we thought nothing of it, for seamen were always walking about. Soon, however, something happened which really did attract our attention. He gradually speeded up his walking pace, then went into a trot and finally, to our utter amazement, took off like the very wind. We turned and watched him as he darted along the path between the Nissen huts and up towards the woods. We stood transfixed, for none of us had ever seen such an impressive display of energy in all our time at Stockheath.

It was as we stood there taking in every detail of the scene that the peace was suddenly shattered by the sound of a strident voice calling, "Stop that man". We looked in the direction from which the call had come and there, in frantic confusion, was a distraught petty officer. The energetic seaman whose athletic skill we had just been admiring was a prisoner who had escaped from his clutches.

It was no good giving chase, for he had already reached the woodland area, with which he was, no doubt, intimately familiar. Something had to be done, however, so every available man was mustered and search parties were sent out in all directions. I was detailed to take my car and patrol the main London road which skirted the other side of the wood, in case he tried to hitch a lift. I did as I was ordered, secretly hoping all the while that I wouldn't see him. Somehow I was on his side. I had no knowledge of his crime, but I didn't want to be the one who caught him.

I went up and down the road, but I never saw him. Nor did any of the other searchers. Of course, he was picked up a few days later. He had made his way back to his home in London, where a reception committee was waiting for him.

The other occasion on which the tranquillity of our life was temporarily disturbed was heralded by a signal which warned us of an impending visit from the Commander-in-Chief, Portsmouth. Nobody knew why such an elevated personage should suddenly wish to inspect our little hide-out. Of the many theories which were put forward, the one which drew the greatest volume of support was that he was coming out to perform the last rites. Whatever the reason, however, it was a situation which called for action.

He could not possibly be allowed to see the entire camp, for most of it was a complete shambles. Thus it was decided to work out a route along which he could be escorted, making sure that he was not allowed to deviate from that fixed course. Everything along that route was to be tidied up and made ship-shape so that our esteemed visitor could not fail to be impressed by the high standard of excellence which we maintained. The Sick Bay and my department figured high on the list, but this gave Doc and me no worries, for they were in impeccable condition. Much work was needed elsewhere, however, and, for the next few days, working parties slaved hard and long, scrubbing and painting and even, in some neglected areas, hacking a path through the undergrowth.

Then, just as it seemed that every possible eventuality had been taken care of, somebody noticed a short sentence, previously overlooked, on that signal from the C-in-C's Office. "Medal ribbons", it said, "will be worn". This caused immediate consternation, for none of us had ever bothered to acquire any such decorations to which we might be entitled, much less to display them on our uniforms. An urgent call to Portsmouth, however, remedied the situation, and, in due course, a petty officer arrived bearing vast quantities of ribbon of all colours, together with all our Service records in order to establish our entitlement to the various decorations. I have to admit that there was a marked scarcity of V.C.s and D.S.C.s, but there was a wide variety of campaign medals, covering all possible theatres of war.

I took my place in the queue knowing that my needs would offer the petty officer no problem at all. Like most Service personnel, it was only campaign medals which came my way, and my total haul numbered just three. I was, therefore, slightly mystified when, after consulting my records, he handed me, in fact, four little pieces of ribbon. I looked at them and tried to identify them. The Defence Medal was easy enough, as was the France and Germany Star. The next one was presumably the Victory Medal, but there was one which was a complete stranger to me.

"What's this?" I asked.

"Burma Star", said the petty officer.

"Burma Star?" I said. "I've never been to Burma."

"Yes, you have", he said impatiently.

"Look", I said. "I know where I've been, and I've certainly never been to Burma. I've never been further east than Normandy."

His patience was beginning to wear a little bit thin and he regarded me with the look of a schoolteacher trying to deal with an awkward child.

"Sir", he said, stressing the word in such a way that it carried more than a hint of sarcasm. "It says here that you served in the Burma campaign. That means, Sir, that you are entitled to the Burma Star. They don't make mistakes about things like that, Sir."

I decided that my best course of action at that point was total surrender so, leaving the queue, I shuffled away clutching my four little pieces of ribbon.

Having acquired our ribbons, we were then confronted with the task of attaching them to our uniforms. They had to be trimmed to a specified size, stitched in a row to a piece of thin card and then sewn on to the left side of one's jacket. This was where the real problems arose, for none of us could claim to be highly skilled at needlecraft. There was only one solution – we would get the Wrens to do it for us. Our little bevy of Wrens occupied a small corner of the camp behind a wire-netting fence in a compound known to one

171

and all as "The Birdcage". We felt sure they would help but, when they learned that there were seventeen of us, they claimed to be too busy sewing on their own ribbons. The best they could offer was to supply the necessary materials. Thus, one of our number was admitted into the Birdcage, from where he later emerged carrying seventeen needles and sufficient thread to circumnavigate the Earth. By the time we had completed our task, there was not much of that thread left.

There was much grunting and groaning as seventeen unsteady pairs of hands struggled to master the intricate task demanded of them. Every little while a burst of strong language would enliven the atmosphere as a missile missed its target and pierced somebody's thumb. It was not until well past midnight that we finished our task and paraded around to show off our handiwork to each other.

The next morning the Commander-in-Chief duly arrived and was greeted with appropriate ceremony. We were all in our appointed places along his route eagerly waiting for a chance to impress him. Sadly, most of us never had that chance. He refused to accept the prescribed route and insisted on going his own way through parts of the camp which we would have preferred him to avoid. All that scrubbing and cleaning had been to no avail. Even worse, our hours of stitching had been completely unnecessary, for very few of us even caught a glimpse of the man. I never learned the final outcome of the inspection, for one more week was destined to bring to an end my connection with Stockheath and, indeed, with the Royal Navy.

My demob number came up and I returned to Portsmouth, where I eventually went through the ritual of my final pay-off and a return to civilian status. They rewarded me with a gratuity of 35 shillings for every month of my service and also a certificate, personally signed by both the Commodore and Captain of HMS *Victory*, which described me as "a competent and conscientious Dental Officer and a good shipmate". I rather liked that personal touch at the end, for it suggested to the uninitiated that we had all been great mates. In truth, however, all past contacts between the three of us had been both brief and formal.

For the next eight weeks I was still to be regarded as a Naval officer, being merely on paid leave. Then, for a further seven years, I was to be listed on the Volunteer Reserve, to face immediate recall if the need should arise. To mark my change of status, however, I was offered certain vestiges of civilian apparel in the shape of either a blue serge suit or more informal attire. I rejected the former, which had a distinct Chaplinesque air about it, and plumped for the sports jacket and flannels. They were not exactly a good fit, but at least they would come in handy for gardening. There was also a trilby hat which, though destined never to be worn, acted as the supreme symbol of my new status. I threw the clothes into the back of my already overloaded car and turned my back for the last time on the Service which I had grown to love. I glanced briefly at the White Ensign hanging limply in the still air and set off back to my roots in Norfolk. The party was over.

My mind was a mixture of conflicting emotions in which only the Past and the Future played a part. The Present was merely a kind of limbo into which I had suddenly drifted and there was certainly no feeling of excitement. My thoughts went back to the pleasures I had found with new people in new places. There were those games of dominoes in that Cornish pub and the love I had shared with Aaron and Rebecca. There was the young padre who couldn't open his mouth without putting his foot in it, and the illicit jewellery business at Lowestoft. But there was also much tragedy – the tiny child in Hackney who never had even one birthday, the airborne slaughter on the streets of London, and the merciless killing on the beaches of Normandy. Now, however, it was all over. From now on, it would be roses all the way. Or would it?

The women of Britain who had taken up wartime jobs would go back to the twin roles of wives and mothers. The men would shed their uniforms and there would be jobs and homes for all of them. We had been promised a Welfare State, under which we would all be looked after "from the Cradle to the Grave". The people of Britain had learned how to become a caring society, and there would be no more poverty and deprivation, no more envy and greed. Or would there?

In the outside world, men of all countries had learned once again that War is a messy, dirty miserable business. The troops would be withdrawn and the refugees would return to their homelands. The price had been paid and, from now on, the people of the World would live at peace with each other.

Or would they?

173

Acknowledgements

Most of the illustrations are from photographs in my own collection, but I am indebted to the following people and organisations for their assistance with additional items:
The British Dental Association (page 10); The London Hospital Medical College (page 19); The Trustees of the Imperial War Museum (pages 68, 69, 129, 135, 143 and 144); and the Director of Music, The Band of H.M. Royal Marines, C-in-C Naval Home Command (page 159).